MEDIA LITERACY

in the K–12 Classroom

Frank W. Baker

International Society for Technology in Education
EUGENE, OREGON • WASHINGTON, DC

Media Literacy in the K–12 Classroom

Frank W. Baker

Director of Book Publishing: *Courtney Burkholder*
Acquisitions Editor: *Jeff V. Bolkan*
Production Editors: *Tina Wells, Lynda Gansel*
Production Coordinator: *Rachel Williams*
Graphic Designer: *Signe Landin*
Copy Editor: *Cecelia Hagen*
Proofreader: *Kathy Hamman*
Indexer: *Wyman Indexing*
Cover Design, Book Design, and Production: *Gwen Thomsen Rhoads*

Library of Congress Cataloging-in-Publication Data

Baker, Frank W.
Media literacy in the K-12 classroom / Frank W. Baker. — 1st ed.
   p. cm.
Includes index.
ISBN 978-1-56484-307-4 (pbk.)
1. Mass media in education—United States. 2. Media literacy—United States. 3. Media literacy—Study and teaching (Elementary) 4. Media literacy—Study and teaching (Secondary) I. Title.
LB1043.B315 2012
373.13'3—dc23

2011034762

First Edition
ISBN: 978-1-56484-307-4
Printed in the United States of America

Cover Images: ©iStockphoto.com/Korhan Karacan (film strip background), ©iStockphoto.com/Julia Savchenko (girl), ©iStockphoto.com/artcyclone (TV), ©iStockphoto.com/slipfloat (car), ©iStockphoto.com/77DZIGN (radio tower), ©iStockphoto.com/Geoffrey Holman (billboard), ©iStockphoto.com/John Takai (food), ©iStockphoto.com/cthoman (cigarette)

ISTE® is a registered trademark of the International Society for Technology in Education.

SUSTAINABLE FORESTRY INITIATIVE   Certified Fiber Sourcing
Label applies to the text stock   www.sfiprogram.org

About ISTE

The International Society for Technology in Education (ISTE) is the trusted source for professional development, knowledge generation, advocacy, and leadership for innovation. ISTE is the premier membership association for educators and education leaders engaged in improving teaching and learning by advancing the effective use of technology in PK–12 and teacher education.

Home of the National Educational Technology Standards (NETS) and ISTE's annual conference and exposition (formerly known as NECC), ISTE represents more than 100,000 professionals worldwide. We support our members with information, networking opportunities, and guidance as they face the challenge of transforming education. To find out more about these and other ISTE initiatives, visit our website at www.iste.org.

As part of our mission, ISTE Book Publishing works with experienced educators to develop and produce practical resources for classroom teachers, teacher educators, and technology leaders. Every manuscript we select for publication is carefully peer reviewed and professionally edited. We value your feedback on this book and other ISTE products. E-mail us at books@iste.org.

International Society for Technology in Education (ISTE)
Washington, DC, Office:
    1710 Rhode Island Ave. NW, Suite 900, Washington, DC 20036-3132
Eugene, Oregon, Office:
    180 West 8th Ave., Suite 300, Eugene, OR 97401-2916
Order Desk: 1.800.336.5191
Order Fax: 1.541.302.3778
Customer Service: orders@iste.org
Book Publishing: books@iste.org
Book Sales and Marketing: booksmarketing@iste.org
Web: www.iste.org

About the Author

Frank W. Baker, a K–12 media educator, has conducted hundreds of workshops with teachers and students. His "Media Literacy Clearinghouse" website has been internationally recognized. He consults for the National Council of Teachers of English as well as the South Carolina Writing Improvement Network.

He is the author of *Political Campaigns and Political Advertising: A Media Literacy Guide* and *Coming Distractions: Questioning Movies,* as well as contributing author of NCTE's *Lesson Plans for Creating Media-Rich Classrooms*; ASCD's *Curriculum 21: Essential Education for a Changing World*; and Telemedia Council's *Visions/Revisions: Moving Forward with Media Education.*

Acknowledgments

Before embarking on writing this book, I posted this question on several school librarians' listservs to which I belong: "What do you need in order to teach media literacy?" In part, I answered my own question when I acknowledged that librarians would certainly need training and resources. Many librarians took the time to provide me with feedback, and to them I say thanks. I have incorporated many of their ideas and suggestions into this text. I know that you, as readers, will need to feel comfortable with the subject before you can begin to teach it; I hope this book is the first step toward that goal.

Frank W. Baker
fbaker1346@aol.com

Contents

CHAPTER 1

WHAT IS MEDIA LITERACY?

It is no longer enough to simply read and write. Students must also become literate in the understanding of visual images.

—Ernest Boyer, former president of the
Carnegie Foundation for the Advancement of Teaching

Communications scholar Marshall McLuhan observed that a fish swimming in the ocean is oblivious to the water. His metaphor is right: we live and swim in a world of media, but we seldom stop to study how the media work or think about their impacts on our lives. Media literacy is designed to do just that and more.

I teach media literacy, a skill set that all students need. By writing this book, I am hoping that you will consider its place in your classroom. But first you need to know what it is and why it is relevant to your students.

Media + Literacy

If we split the phrase *media literacy* apart, we come up with two words: media (the plural form of medium) and literacy (the ability to read, write, and comprehend). We all know what the various media are, especially our students. Literacy is one of the driving forces of education. We want students who can read, write, think critically, and contribute to society.

In today's education system, literacy is taught primarily through the printed word (books, magazines, etc.). Educators understand that students require the ability to read, analyze, interpret, deconstruct, and create printed words. However, photographers, filmmakers, advertisers, and other media makers know that there are languages and rules that set their media apart from the printed word—and it is these rules that media literacy aims to teach. Filmmaker George Lucas wants educators to value and teach these rules:

> If students aren't taught the language of sound and images, shouldn't they be considered as illiterate as if they left college without being able to read and write? (George Lucas, quoted in Daly, 2004, para. 7)

Simply put, media literacy is the ability to understand how the media work, how they convey meaning. Media literacy also involves critical thinking about the thousands of media messages we are bombarded with on a daily basis.

One of my favorite definitions of media literacy comes from Canada:

> Media literacy is concerned with helping students develop an informed and critical understanding of the nature of mass media, the techniques used by them, and the impact of these techniques. More specifically, it is education that aims to increase the students' understanding and enjoyment of how the media work, how they produce meaning, how they are organized, and how they construct reality. Media literacy also aims to provide students with the ability to create media products. (Ontario Ministry of Education, 1989, pp. 6–7)

Many educators know how to teach with media; unfortunately, not many know how to teach about the media. In one of my recent workshops, I asked a large group of secondary social studies teachers if they could teach history without images, and they all said no. When I asked how many of them teach "visual literacy," not one person responded in the affirmative.

Although media literacy has been around since the 1960s, many educators still don't understand what it is and where it fits into the K–12 curriculum. The American education system has not yet fully embraced it. But there are signs that this is changing.

In 1998, I created the Media Literacy Clearinghouse website (www.frankwbaker.com) because I wanted to offer educators a one-stop venue for resources that would help them better understand media literacy and its place in the classroom. The center of the homepage is divided into three columns, each with background, readings, lesson plans, and resources. The left column contains some of the major media literacy concepts. The center column is divided into curriculum areas. The right column contains some of the more popular pages and resources that teachers have told me they like to use.

> **Media Literacy Clearinghouse Website**
>
> One-stop venue for media literacy resources: www.frankwbaker.com

I hope you will take some time to explore the site. A few words of advice: it is easy to get lost on a web page with hundreds of embedded links. Choose a topic (e.g., advertising) or a curriculum discipline (e.g., English) that interests you, and explore the resources on those pages.

Media literacy encourages us to consider the world of our students—their media, their popular culture—as the hook to get their attention and get them engaged, while also meeting essential teaching standards. On my website, you will find ideas for teaching with and about visual images, film, television, advertising, and more. You will find topics as diverse as advertising, bias, journalism, news, parody, propaganda, and much, much more. I hope, after reading this book and considering its recommendations, you will also feel more comfortable helping your students become critical thinkers and viewers in a media-saturated world.

Media literacy is recognized as a set of new skills all students need to succeed. The Partnership for 21st Century Skills (www.p21.org) defines media literacy in terms of two skill sets—analysis and production—that students need to acquire.

Analyze Media

- Understand both how and why media messages are constructed and for what purposes

- Examine how individuals interpret messages differently, how values and points of view are included or excluded, and how media can influence beliefs and behaviors

- Apply a fundamental understanding of the ethical/legal issues surrounding the access and use of media

Create Media Products

- Understand and utilize the most appropriate media-creation tools, characteristics, and conventions

- Understand and effectively utilize the most appropriate expressions and interpretations in diverse, multicultural environments. (www.p21.org/index. php?option=com_content&task=view&id=349&Itemid=120)

The Partnership for 21st Century Skills (P21), working with teachers from all disciplines, has produced ICT (information, communication, and technology) curriculum skills maps, all of which make specific recommendations to teachers who want to revise their instruction for the challenges of the 21st century. Included in each of these ICT maps is a page devoted to "media literacy." To read the map for your discipline, go to www.p21.org/index. php?option=com_content&task=view&id=31.

The Importance of Analysis

Many teachers (and students) have become enamored of small camcorders because they are inexpensive and easy to use. They are increasingly being incorporated into instruction. Although I applaud this move, learning how to use a camera, understanding editing techniques, and incorporating video into a project is only half of the equation. Students, in this example, are only creators and producers. Teachers should also be teaching their students how to analyze media productions. When we take time to help students analyze media messages, they learn to understand the underlying techniques that influence them every day, and they become healthy skeptics.

In her book *Reading the Media in High School* media scholar Renee Hobbs (2007) says she found that teaching students to analyze media messages also helped them become better readers of print material.

Put simply, Hobbs has found that analysis combined with production translates into effective media literacy practice. Teachers who will teach it need to engage their students in both activities. But media literacy is much more than just analysis and production.

Media literacy is also:

- a set of skills, knowledge, and abilities

- an awareness of personal media habits

- an understanding of how media works (production, economics)

- an appreciation of media's power/influence

- the ability to discern, critically question/view

- an understanding of how meaning is created in media

- a healthy skepticism

- access to media

- the ability to produce and create media

What media literacy is not:

- media bashing: it is not designed to say media is bad

- protection against media we might disagree with

- just about television: it offers many opportunities to analyze and produce new media and technology

- limited to video production

- how to use audio-visual equipment

- only teaching with media; it is also teaching *about* the media

Media literacy is not a separate course; instead, it is a lens though which we see and understand our media-saturated world. It is also a teaching strategy that should be incorporated into every course.

Whenever teachers use a photograph, a film clip, a commercial, an educational video, an audio recording, or a snippet from the news, they have an opportunity to engage students in better understanding:

- how that media message was created and constructed

- who the intended audience is

- what techniques might be used to engage, inform, persuade, and educate

- who or what might be omitted and why

- who benefits/profits from the message being told in this way

- what biases might be inherent

- what stereotypes are promoted

- and more

These and other questions are considered crucial to media literacy education. Questioning media messages, which many of us have not been trained to do, is one of the major strategies that can be employed in teaching about the media.

Tessa Jolls, the president of the Center for Media Literacy (CML), agrees:

> It is our dream that by the time they graduate from high school, all students will be able to apply the Five Key Questions almost without thinking. ... Practicing and mastering the Five Key Questions leads to an adult understanding of how media are created, what their purposes are, and how to accept or reject their messages. (www.medialit.org/five-key-questions-can-change-world)

CML's Five Core Concepts

The Center recommends students become familiar with the five core concepts as well as the corresponding critical-thinking questions:

1. All media messages are "constructed."

2. Media messages are constructed using a creative language with its own rules.

3. Different people experience the same message differently.

4. Media have embedded values and points of view.

5. Most media messages are organized to gain profit and/or power. (Thoman & Jolls, 2003, p. 18)

CML's Five Key (Deconstruction) Questions

1. Who created this message?

2. What creative techniques are used to attract my attention?

3. How might different people understand this message differently from me?

4. What lifestyles, values, and points of view are represented in, or omitted from, this message?

5. Why was this message sent? (Thoman & Jolls, 2003, p. 18)

CML's core concepts and key questions are explained and explored in Chapter 2.

NAMLE's Key Questions to Ask When Analyzing Media Messages

The National Association of Media Literacy Education (NAMLE) recently recommended the following longer list of questions for all students to use when considering media messages:

Authorship: Who made this message?

Purpose: Why was this made? Who is the target audience (and how do you know)?

Economics: Who paid for this?

Impact: Who might benefit from this message? Who might be harmed by it? Why might this message matter to me?

Response: What kinds of actions might I take in response to this message?

Content: What is this about (and what makes you think that)? What ideas, values, information, and/or points of view are overt? Implied? What is left out of this message that might be important to know?

Techniques: What techniques are used? Why were those techniques used? How do they communicate the message?

Interpretations: How might different people understand this message differently? What is my interpretation of this and what do I learn about myself from my reaction or interpretation?

Context: When was this made? Where or how was it shared with the public?

Credibility: Is this fact, opinion, or something else? How credible is this (and what makes you think that)? What are the sources of the information, ideas, or assertions?

Source: NAMLE, Core Principles of Media Literacy Education (http://namle.net/publications/core-principles/).

NAMLE (formerly AMLA) provides a one-page handout of these key questions in PDF form (http://namle.net/wp-content/uploads/2009/09/NAMLEKeyQuestions0708.pdf). Post them in your classroom, project them on a whiteboard or overhead projector, and use them every time you teach a media literacy lesson. The more you use them, the more familiar your students will be with questioning media messages, whether they emanate from television, Google, or Twitter.

Media Literacy and Curriculum Standards/Disciplines

In 1998, while attending a National Media Literacy Conference, I was struck with an idea: if we want young people to become media literate, perhaps we should examine each state's curriculum standards and look for evidence of media literacy. That's exactly what I did. Rutgers University media professor Robert Kubey and I worked together, deciding to concentrate our media literacy search in three major curriculum areas: English language arts (ELA), social studies, and health.

The results of our study (published in October 1999 in the trade publication *Education Week*) surprised us and most of those working in the field of media literacy: elements of media literacy could be found in almost every state's standards. The phrase "media literacy" is not often used, but when we examine those three disciplines, it becomes clear that certain words and phrases are common to almost all state standards.

For example, in English language arts, there is the phrase "nonprint texts": this refers to television, radio, motion pictures, and more. In addition, "persuasive techniques" are included in most ELA standards (and examining advertising and commercials is one way of using the media to teach students how to identify those techniques). Bias as a concept is also taught in ELA classrooms when students study author's bias along with media bias. Many teachers who use film are helping their students understand narrative structure, symbolism, camera angles, and more (Kubey & Baker, 1999).

In *The English Teacher's Companion*, author Jim Burke (2007) urges English teachers to embrace media: "Movies, advertisements, and all other visual media are tools teachers need to use and media we must master if we are to maintain our credibility in the coming years" (p. 341).

Texas, for example, has made media literacy part of its reading standard: "Students use comprehension skills to analyze how words, images, graphics, and sounds work together in various forms to impact meaning."

NCTE Recommendations

The National Council of Teachers of English has consistently recommended media literacy education. Resolutions and position statements, some dating back to the 1970s, have recognized the power and influence of media texts on young readers. Many states have revised their ELA standards based on NCTE's recommendations.

Expectations for fifth grade English language arts and reading students in Texas and ELA standards for sixth and seventh grade students in Connecticut are shown below:

State Standards for ELA

Texas

5th Grade Reading/Media Literacy (24)

(A) explain how messages conveyed in various forms of media are presented differently (e.g., documentaries, online information, televised news);

(B) consider the difference in techniques used in media (e.g., commercials, documentaries, news);

(C) identify the point of view of media presentations;

(D) analyze various digital media venues for levels of formality and informality. (www.sharongullett.net/elateks)

Connecticut

6th Grade

1.25 Evaluate the credibility, accuracy and bias of informational text, including Internet sites, electronic recordings, visuals and other technology resources. (www.perma-bound.com/state-standards. do?state=CT&subject=language-arts&gradeLevel=6)

7th Grade

1.16 Evaluate how authors, illustrators and filmmakers express political and social issues. (www.perma-bound.com/state-standards. do?state=CT&subject=language-arts&gradeLevel=7)

In social studies, many states refer to the rise of mass media (radio, TV, film) in American history. Propaganda is also commonly found in many history standards. The role of the media in the political campaign process is another way teachers can address media literacy, by studying how candidates use the media to reach citizens, especially during election times.

In 2009, the National Council of the Social Studies (NCSS) approved a position statement on the importance of media literacy. The statement appears below:

Social Studies Statement on Media Literacy
NCSS Position Statement Media literacy is a pedagogical approach promoting the use of diverse types of media and information communication technology (from crayons to webcams) to question the roles of media and society and the multiple meanings of all types of messages. Analysis of media content is combined with inquiry into the medium. This approach is analytical and skill-based. Thus media literacy integrates the process of critical inquiry with the creation of media as students examine, create, and disseminate their own alternative images, sounds, and thoughts. (www.socialstudies.org/positions/medialiteracy, para. 10)

In health studies, students learn how media influence health behaviors. Standard 2 of the National Health Education Standards (NHES), available from the Centers for Disease Control and Prevention (CDC), references the media specifically:

NHES Standard
Standard 2 Students will analyze the influence of family, peers, culture, media, technology, and other factors on health behaviors. (www.cdc.gov/healthyyouth/sher/standards)

Examples from Other States

In Colorado, the health standard for middle and high school says:

> Students should be able to identify and explain how the media may influence behaviors and decisions.

In South Carolina, high school students

> examine ways that media messages and marketing techniques
> influence alcohol, tobacco, and other drug use.

The state of Georgia's standard says students will

> identify ways various forms of media, such as movies, glorify
> drug use.

And in Missouri, the standard reads students will

> evaluate the idealized body image and elite performance levels
> portrayed by the media and determine the influence of a young
> adult's self concept, goal setting and health decisions.

Other Disciplines

Some of the same concepts of media literacy are also covered in many of our arts classrooms, where students begin to appreciate the techniques used to create productions. Understanding visual literacy by studying painting, for example, is a skill that can transfer to the analysis of still images, such as photographs, posters, and other visual representations.

Media literacy is also a fixture in many other disciplines, even though it is not referred to as such. In science classrooms, the centerpiece is on inquiry—asking questions. More recently, there has been a push to increase the "science literacy" of students and the general public.

Many science teachers use videos to teach complex topics; others use popular films as examples of addressing biology, space science, astronomy, chemistry, and physics. Every time an educator uses a video with students, there is yet another opportunity to engage them in critical thinking and viewing.

In math classrooms, teachers could expose students to the manner in which news providers use numbers and the graphical representation of numbers. Key media literacy concepts (explored further in the next chapter) are great ways to get students thinking about how numbers are used by news writers and reporters.

Why Teach Media Literacy?

I have described media literacy as a lens through which we see and understand our world. Educated people who are media literate are more likely to be able to spot propaganda, question marketing, understand stereotypes, and identify their own biases as well as those of authors. Without media literacy, more people will be fooled because they don't understand how they're being manipulated.

Today, more attention than ever is being given to the amount of time young people spend in front of the screens (televisions, computers, phones). Research tells us that the more time young people spend watching television, the worse their grades are. Furthermore, increased screen time has been linked to junk food consumption, obesity, attention deficit disorder, and a host of other health effects. Pediatricians are now asking parents about their children's media habits, just as they would ask about the food they eat and the liquids they drink.

Every holiday season, millions of Americans head to stores to buy toys. Their purchases are often based on toys advertised on television, and because the majority of these young people have never had any media literacy education, they're not able to see through the deceptive and manipulative practices of commercial producers that make toys look better than they really are. (More about toy advertising and what teachers can do is discussed later in this book.)

In the U.S., millions of us go to the voting booths every four years and elect the next president. More than likely we will have seen, on television and online, one of the candidate's commercials (created by slick advertising executives) designed to make us feel good about the candidate. These ads are produced by the same people who sell us toothpaste. Without a media literacy education, we might elect someone based on their looks and the production values of a 30-second commercial.

Large and influential corporations maintain public relations and marketing staffs that are ready to go to work at a moment's notice if and when needed. Media observer Jean Kilbourne (2000) notes: "Huge and powerful industries—alcohol, tobacco, junk food, diet, guns—depend upon a media-illiterate population." Kilbourne stresses the importance of "using the tools of media education" to help us "understand, analyze, interpret, [and] expose hidden agendas and manipulation" (p. 305). It's critically important for young people today to know who creates these slick messages and to be able to see through their creative and persuasive techniques.

Product placement describes the multimillion-dollar practice of placing real products inside the plots of prime time television shows and popular motion pictures. Why is this happening? More of us are "zapping" the commercials with our DVRs and TiVos. Advertisers know that audiences aren't watching the ads, so their answer is to put the products inside the shows, where we will be sure to see them.

In 2010, the MacArthur Foundation released *Kids and Credibility*, a major report by Andrew Flanagin and Miriam Metzger, examining young people's use and understanding of information found on the Internet. It was widely believed, but not yet proved, that students who use the Internet for their homework and other research believe the web to be today's encyclopedia—containing all the information (and answers) to questions they might need for school and beyond.

The *Kids and Credibility* report confirmed our worst fears. The survey of young people ages 11–18 revealed that 89% of them believe that "some" to "a lot" of online information is "believable" (Flanagin & Metzger, 2010). The full report is available at http://mitpress.mit.edu/books/full_pdfs/Kids_and_Credibility.pdf.

The Benefits of Media Literacy Education

The Center for Media Literacy says teaching media literacy skills to young people helps them acquire an empowering set of navigational skills that enable them to do the following:

- *Access* information from a variety of sources.

- *Analyze* and *explore* how messages are "constructed"—whether print, verbal, visual or multimedia.

- *Evaluate* media's explicit and implicit messages against one's own ethical, moral, and/or democratic principles.

- *Express* or *create* their own messages using a variety of media tools. (www.medialit.org/reading-room/empowerment-through-education)

The College Board, in its English Language Arts Framework (2006), also identifies what it means for students to be media literate:

1. Students who are media literate communicators demonstrate knowledge and understanding of the ways people use media in their personal and public lives.

2. Media literate students know and understand the complex relationships among audiences and media content.

3. Media literate students know and understand that media content is produced within social and cultural contexts.

4. Media literate students know and understand the commercial nature of media and demonstrate the ability to use media to communicate to specific audiences.

5. Media literate students understand, interpret, analyze, and evaluate media communication.

6. Media literate students use a variety of technological and informational resources (e.g., libraries, databases, computer networks, video) to gather and synthesize information and to create and communicate knowledge.

7. Media literate students understand, interpret, analyze, and evaluate media communication. (www.collegeboard.com/prod_downloads/about/association/academic/EnglishFramework.pdf, p. 55)

For all of these reasons and more, media literacy education is vitally important. It equips young people with the skills they need not only to question media messages, but also to be critical and competent communicators and producers.

CHAPTER 2

TEACHING MEDIA LITERACY

Without an understanding of media grammars, we cannot hope to achieve a contemporary awareness of the world in which we live.

—Carpenter & McLuhan, 1960, p. xii

Pedagogy and Principles of Teaching Media Literacy

In Chapter 1, we introduced the media literacy core concepts and key critical thinking (deconstruction) questions. Becoming familiar with both is important for teachers and students in order to understand media literacy and how the media work.

The Center for Media Literacy's founder, Elizabeth Thoman, stresses the importance of critical inquiry, and she goes on to say it's not just asking questions, but asking the right questions: "at the heart of media literacy is the principle of inquiry" (Thoman, 1993).

Bill Yousman of the Media Education Foundation sums it up best:

> It's not about teaching kids how to watch TV. … It's about teaching them to watch TV critically. In our schools we take it for granted that we should teach children how to analyze a poem in great detail. But in fact, children will be exposed to many more ads and sitcoms and video games and Hollywood movies in their lives than poetry. (Asking the Right Questions: The Power of Media Literacy, www.washingtonpost.com/wp-dyn/content/article/2006/08/04/AR2006080400226.html)

In Chapter 3, Visual Literacy, I recommend some images from history and popular culture as starting points to get our students thinking and questioning. When using an image, for example, I will strip away the caption (the context) in order to get students to simply focus on the image itself.

We know that young people are exposed to literally thousands of media messages daily. Even in school they are not immune from marketing and advertising. When teachers take the time to become familiar with youth media and popular culture, they will find it is the hook to engaging their students in learning, while at the same time meeting teaching standards and other learning objectives. So regardless of the medium (TV, radio, film, newspapers, magazines, Internet) or the method (advertising, bias, propaganda, stereotypes, etc.) the concepts combined with the questions are essential starting points for analysis, deconstruction, interpretation and more.

Expansion and Explanation of Key Deconstruction Questions

The chart below is based on the Center for Media Literacy's five key questions for consumers and producers.

Media Deconstruction/Construction Framework by Center for Media Literacy (CML)		
Core Concept	**Key Deconstruction Question**	**Construction Question**
1. All media messages are "constructed."	Who created this message?	What am I authoring?
2. Media messages are constructed using a creative language with its own rules.	What creative techniques are used to attract my attention?	Does my message reflect understanding in format, creativity and technology?
3. Different people experience the same media message differently.	How might different people understand this message differently from me?	Is my message engaging and compelling for my target audience?
4. Media have embedded values and points of view.	What lifestyles, values, and points of view are represented in, or omitted from, this message?	Have I clearly and consistently framed values, lifestyles and points of view in my content?
5. Most media messages are organized to gain profit and/or power.	Why is this message being sent?	Have I communicated my purpose effectively?

Source: CML Media LitKit, CML's Five Key Questions and Core Concepts (Q/Tips) for Consumers and Producers (Center for Media Literacy, 2009, www.medialit.com).

Key Words and Key Questions

The key words associated with the five CML key questions are authorship, format, audience, content, and purpose.

CML Key Question 1 speaks to **authorship**. The CML suggests these additional guiding questions be considered:

What kind of "text" is it?

What are the various elements (building blocks) that make up the whole?

How similar or different is it to others of the same genre?

Which technologies are used in its creation?

How would it be different in a different medium?

What choices were made that might have been made differently?

How many people did it take to create this message?

What are their various jobs? (Thoman & Jolls, 2003, p. 23)

CML Key Question 2 speaks to **format**. These questions are recommended:

What do you notice … about the way the message is constructed?

- Colors? Shapes? Size?
- Sounds? Words? Silence?
- Props? Sets? Clothing?
- Movement?
- Composition? Lighting?

Where is the camera? What is the viewpoint?

How is the story told visually? What are people doing?

Are there any visual symbols? Metaphors?

What's the emotional appeal? Persuasive devices?

What makes it seem "real?" (Thoman & Jolls, 2003, p. 24)

CML Key Question 3 speaks to **audience**; consider these questions:

Have you ever experienced anything like this?

How close does it come to what you experienced in real life?

What did you learn from this media text? What did you learn *about yourself* from experiencing the media text?

What did you learn from other people's response—and their experience?

How many other interpretations could there be? How could we hear about them?

How can you explain the different responses?

Are other viewpoints just as valid as mine? (Thoman & Jolls, 2003, p. 25)

CML Key Question 4 addresses **content** with these questions:

How is the human person characterized? What kinds of behaviors/consequences are depicted?

What type of person is the reader/watcher/listener invited to identify with?

What questions come to mind as you watch/read/listen?

What ideas or values are being "sold" to us in this message?

What political ideas are communicated in the message?

What judgments or statements are made about how we treat other people?

What is the overall worldview?

Are any ideas or perspectives left out? How would you find what's missing? (Thoman & Jolls, 2003, p. 26)

CML Key Question 5 addresses **purpose** with these questions:

> Who's in control of the creation and transmission of this message?
>
> Why are they sending it? How do you know?
>
> Who are they sending it to? How do you know?
>
> Who is served by, profits from, or benefits from the message?
>
> - the public?
> - private interests?
> - individuals?
> - institutions?
>
> Who wins? Who loses? Who decides?
>
> What economic decisions may have influenced the message's construction or transmission? (Thoman & Jolls, 2003, p. 27)

Additional Deconstruction Questions

Here are additional questions for clarifying the **purpose** (Key Question 5):

> What's being sold in this message?
>
> What's being told?
>
> Who profits from this message?
>
> Who pays for it?

Getting our students to become critical thinkers (and viewers) by questioning media messages is an important goal. Over time, I've developed and used the following series of critical thinking questions:

1. Who is the producer/storyteller of the message?

2. What is the producer's purpose/motive/agenda?

3. Who is the intended (primary) target audience?

    - How do you know?

    - Is there another (secondary) audience?

4. What does the message say? How does it say it?

5. How do you know what the message means?

6. What format/medium does the producer use?

7. What are the advantages of the format/medium?

8. What methods/techniques does the producer use to make the message attractive/believable?

9. What lifestyle is portrayed in the message? What clues tell you?

10. Who makes money or benefits from the message?

11. Who/what is left out of the message?

12. Whose interests are served by telling/showing the message in a particular way?

13. Do you agree with the message?

14. How might different people interpret the message differently?

15. After studying the message, what do you know, what do you not know, and what would you like to know?

16. Where can you go to verify the information in the message or get more reliable information?

17. What can you do with the information you have obtained from the message?

Pedagogical Concepts

The five core concepts and corresponding key questions developed by the Center for Media Literacy are just one of the models for teaching media literacy. Another framework for teaching media literacy is the Media Literacy Triangle (Figure 2.1), developed by Eddie Dick of the Scottish Film Council and included in Rick Shepherd's "Elementary Media Education: The Perfect Curriculum" (1992). This model drives and supports curriculum development and learning outcomes.

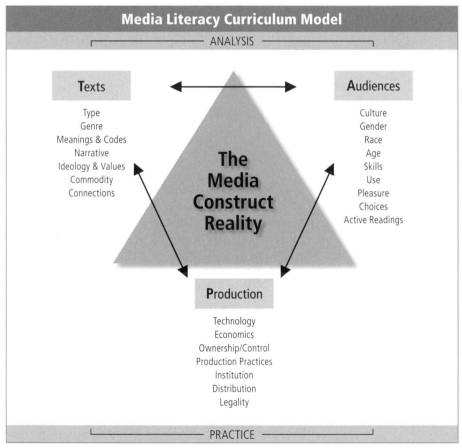

FIGURE 2.1 Media literacy triangle.

Source: Dick, in Shepherd, 1992.

A *text* is any media product we wish to examine. Anyone who receives a media text is a member of an *audience*. *Production* refers to everything that goes into the making of a media text (Shepherd, 1992).

Most educators agree that effective media literacy pedagogy must involve the use of authentic media texts, so that students are actively engaged in not only analyzing media, but creating it as well. Let's take advertising as an example. An elementary educator might start by having his or her students begin to identify and be aware of signs.

Students might draw five different types of sign. The teacher might introduce a billboard as one type of sign—thus students begin to be aware that signs are ads and use colors, words, and images to get attention.

A middle grades educator might have his or her students engage in a semester-long survey of their environment, identifying where ads are located, including at home and at school. Students could use digital cameras to photograph the ads, making notes of locations, demographics, techniques of persuasion, and more. Using magazines found at school or at home, students could conduct a "content analysis," noting which products are pitched and who is being targeted. A high school teacher might take students into the real world of advertising. They might view episodes of AMC's "Mad Men" to get a feel for how ad agencies pitched campaigns in the 1960s. Students might research how a particular product or candidate might have been marketed then and compare it to how the product or person is (or would be) marketed now, noticing the similarities and the differences.

The teacher could invite a retired advertising executive who could discuss and help dispel some of the myths portrayed in the "Mad Men" series. Another great advertising activity would be to engage students in learning how to "read" an ad, analyzing and deconstructing the words, images, layout, and inferred and subtext messages, as well as the economics behind it. The teacher might then have students create their own ads by using online tools, such as Glogster or VoiceThread, or by simply using construction paper and markers. It is the combination of analysis plus production that makes media literacy education so effective.

Most schools today understand that learning must also engage the student in higher order thinking skills (HOTS). A major element in HOTS is learning to ask questions about what we see, read, and hear. Media literacy, as we have seen, certainly fits in here with its emphasis on "critical inquiry."

Bloom's Digital Taxonomy		
Key Terms	HOTS Higher Order Thinking Skills	Communication Spectrum
Creating — verbs →	designing, constructing, planning, producing, inventing, devising, making, programming, filming, animating, blogging, video blogging, mixing, re-mixing, wiki-ing, publishing, videocasting, podcasting, directing, broadcasting	Collaborating Moderating Negotiating Debating
Evaluating — verbs →	checking, hypothesizing, critiquing, experimenting, judging, testing, detecting, monitoring, blog commenting, reviewing, posting, moderating, collaborating, networking, refactoring, testing	Net meeting Skyping Videoconferencing
Analyzing — verbs →	comparing, organizing, deconstructing, attributing, outlining, finding, structuring, integrating, mashing, linking, validating, reverse engineering, cracking, media clipping	Reviewing Questioning Replying
Applying — verbs →	implementing, carrying out, using, executing, running, loading, playing, operating, hacking, uploading, sharing, editing	Replying Posting & Blogging Networking
Understanding — verbs →	interpreting, summarizing, inferring, paraphrasing, classifying, comparing, explaining, exemplifying, advanced searches, Boolean searches, blog journalizing, twittering, categorizing, tagging, commenting, annotating, subscribing	Contributing Chatting emailing
Remembering — verbs →	recognizing, listing, describing, identifying, retrieving, naming, locating, finding, bullet pointing, highlighting, bookmarking, social networking, social bookmarking, favoriting/local bookmarking, searching, googling	Twittering/ Microblogging Instant messaging Texting
LOTS Lower Order Thinking Skills		

FIGURE 2.2 Bloom's Digital Taxonomy (A. Churches, 2008).

Since the mid 1950s, educators have relied on and put into practice Benjamin Bloom's Taxonomy of Learning. The verbs of Bloom's taxonomy describe the skills students should know to be effective learners of knowledge. Over time, Bloom's taxonomy has changed to reflect many of the changes in education thinking. Most recently, a Bloom's Digital Taxonomy has emerged; at the top of the higher order thinking skills sits the verb "creating." And what would students create? In this model (see Figure 2.2), students are creating media, such as film, video, blogs, podcasts (audio), and more.

Why Study the Media?

Today's students spend much of their waking time connected to the media. Among young people ages 8–18, the average amount time spent with all media (TV, music, computers, videogames, print, and movies) is 7 hours and 38 minutes per day; however, "today's youth pack a total of 10 hours and 45 minutes worth of media content into those daily 7 $^1/_2$ hours" (Rideout, Foehr, & Roberts, 2010, p. 2). This figure actually shocked researchers for the Kaiser Family Foundation when they announced the latest data in January 2010. They had expected time spent viewing TV, for example, to be displaced by new media. It was not.

So young people are enamored with media. How can we, as educators, take advantage of their love of media? Tap into it. When we recognize the media and popular culture of our students and incorporate it into instruction, we demonstrate that we value their media and its connections with learning.

One of the things all educators need to acknowledge is that media are also texts. This book will help you begin to teach with and about the media. Currently media analysis and deconstruction activities are not common in textbooks. This book will help you, and your students, begin to recognize the importance and relevance of media literacy and its place in the classroom.

A Framework for Teaching Media Literacy

One popular framework to use with students to help them better understand media and media literacy is the TAP Questioning Model. In Figures 2.1 and 2.3, TAP represents three sides of a triangle and stands for text, audience, and production.

> **Text** is typically associated with something in print. However, text can also be a film, a TV show, an advertisement, a radio program, a photograph, or a video game.

> **Audience** is the particular demographic that each text is designed specifically for.

> **Production** is the process of making (putting together) or creating media texts.

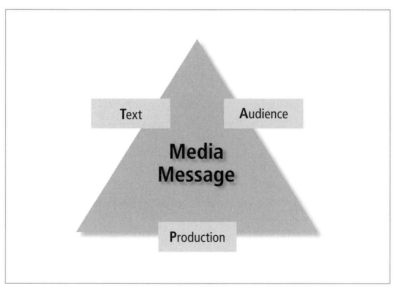

FIGURE 2.3 TAP Questioning Model.

Students could study a media text by applying a specific list of questions. Take a look at the following questions developed by David Considine and used in Diane Marks' (2009) materials for her course at Appalachian State University:

Text

What kind of media work is this (magazine, T-shirt, poster, etc.)?

In what ways does this media work tell a story?

What type or category of story is it?

Does it follow a formula?

What are the codes and conventions used?

What are the characters like?

Are there any stereotypes?

What values are being promoted?

How do I know this?

Whose point of view do the values represent?

Are my values represented?

Why or why not?

Audience

Who is the target audience for this media work?

How can I tell?

How and why does this media work appeal to its audience?

How does this media work appeal to me?

What things do I like and dislike?

In what ways do people use or consume the media work to make it more enjoyable?

What is the message (implicit and explicit)?

Production

Who produced this media work and for what purpose?

How can I influence the production of this kind of media work?

How is this text distributed or sold to the public? Who profits?

How was the text made?

What production techniques are used?

What rules and laws affect the media work (copyright, running time, trademarks, etc.)?

How could I produce a similar media work? (Adapted from Marks, 2009)

The BFI (UK) Model

The British Film Institute (BFI) has codified media education "curriculum statements" in terms of conceptual understanding. These key aspects have had a global influence beyond the United Kingdom (Buckingham, 2001). In New Zealand, for instance, media education has developed around the following BFI key concepts.

BFI's Original Key Concepts of Media Literacy	
Media audiences	**Who is watching?** How audiences are identified, constructed, addressed and reached; how audiences find, choose, consume and respond to media texts.
Media technologies	**How do they do that?** What kinds of technologies are available, to whom, how to use them, the differences they make to the production process as well as the final product.
Media agencies/ownership	**Who made/owns what?** Who produces the text; [has] roles in production process, media institutions, economics and ideologies, intentions and results.
Media languages	**How do they convey meaning?** How the media produces meanings; codes and conventions; narrative structure.
Media categories	**What is it?** Different media (television, radio, cinema etc); forms (documentary, advertising etc); genres, other ways of categorizing text; how categorization relates to understanding.
Media representation	**How are things, places and people portrayed in the media?** The relation between media texts and the actual places, people, events, ideas; stereotyping and its consequences.

Source: New Zealand Ministry of Education's bilingual website, Te Kete Ipurangi (2011), http://media-studies.tki.org.nz/Teaching-media-studies/Media-concepts/Chart-of-key-concepts (Bowker, BFI, 1991).

Canadian Key Concepts and Approach

In 1989, the Ministry of Education in Ontario published the influential *Media Literacy Resource Guide*, designed to provide educators with the necessary background on teaching media literacy. In this guide, eight key concepts were introduced and continue to be the framework for educators in the provinces of Canada.

Canada's Original Eight Key Concepts for Media Literacy	
1. All media are construction.	The media do not present simple reflections of external reality. Rather, they present carefully crafted constructions that reflect many decisions and result from many determining factors. Media literacy works towards deconstructing these constructions, taking them apart to show how they are made.
2. The media construct versions of reality.	The media are responsible for the majority of the observations and experiences from which we build up our personal understandings of the world and how it works. Much of our view of reality is based on media messages that have been pre-constructed and have attitudes, interpretations and conclusions already built in. The media, to a great extent, give us our sense of reality.
3. Audiences negotiate meaning in the media.	The media provide us with much of the material upon which we build our picture of reality, and we all "negotiate" meaning according to individual factors: personal needs and anxieties, the pleasures or troubles of the day, racial and sexual attitudes, family and cultural background, and so forth.
4. Media have commercial implications.	Media literacy aims to encourage an awareness of how the media are influenced by commercial considerations, and how these affect content, technique and distribution. Most media production is a business, and must therefore make a profit. Questions of ownership and control are central: a relatively small number of individuals control what we watch, read and hear in the media.
5. Media contain ideological and value messages.	All media products are advertising, in some sense, in that they proclaim values and ways of life. Explicitly or implicitly, the mainstream media convey ideological messages about such issues as the nature of the good life, the virtue of consumerism, the role of women, the acceptance of authority, and unquestioning patriotism.
6. Media have social and political implications.	The media have great influence on politics and on forming social change. Television can greatly influence the election of a national leader on the basis of image. The media involve us in concerns such as civil rights issues, famines in Africa, and the AIDS epidemic. They give us an intimate sense of national issues and global concerns, so that we become citizens of Marshall McLuhan's "Global Village."
7. Form and content are closely related in the media.	As Marshall McLuhan noted, each medium has its own grammar and codifies reality in its own particular way. Different media will report the same event, but create different impressions and messages.
8. Each medium has a unique aesthetic form.	Just as we notice the pleasing rhythms of certain pieces of poetry or prose, so we ought to be able to enjoy the pleasing forms and effects of the different media.

Source: The Association for Media Literacy, Toronto, Ontario.

Center for Media Literacy and the U.S. Approach

In the 1970s, the Center for Media & Values was created (later becoming the Center for Media Literacy). CML, "the Center," was, for the longest time, the main proponent of media literacy education in U.S. schools, churches, and after-school settings. CML was at the forefront of media literacy education by promoting the Five Core Concepts as a beginning framework for studying and understanding media messages. The concepts included ideas previously promoted by media educators in the United Kingdom, Canada, Australia, and New Zealand. These have become universal in media literacy education circles.

Teachers could and should post these in the classroom, use them as handouts, and begin to help students understand media literacy using this approach.

Center for Media Literacy Five Core Concepts	
1. All media messages are "constructed."	Whether it's the morning newspaper, a hip-hop video, or the image of a young woman on a magazine cover: they're all constructed.
2. Media messages are constructed using a creative language with its own rules.	Each new medium or technology brings a new vocabulary, for example the language of film.
3. Different people experience the same media message differently.	The headline "Paris Liberated" might be interpreted by an older person to mean World War II, but might also mean "Paris Hilton getting out of jail" to someone younger.
4. Media have embedded values and points of view.	The image of President Bush with a dunce cap, sitting on a stool in the corner of the room (on the cover of *Rolling Stone* magazine) reveals much about the point-of-view of the publication.
5. Most media messages are organized to gain profit and/or power.	In 1983, 50 corporations controlled the majority of American media; by 2004 that number was 4. What are the ramifications if only four companies control much of what you see, read and hear?

Source for core concepts: Thoman & Jolls, 2003, p. 18.

Since the introduction of CML's core concepts and critical thinking questions, many other organizations have, in their own ways, recognized the importance of teaching with and about the media. In 1996, the National Council of Teachers of English (NCTE) passed a resolution urging language arts teachers to consider the importance of bringing visual texts into the classroom. The resolution said:

> Viewing and visually representing (defined in the NCTE/IRA *Standards for the English Language Arts*) are a part of our growing consciousness of how people gather and share information. Teachers and students need to expand their appreciation of the power of print and nonprint texts. Teachers should guide students in constructing meaning through creating and viewing nonprint texts. (www.ncte.org/positions/ statements/visualformofliteracy)

> **Origin of CML's Five Core Concepts**
>
> The Five Core Concepts have been around quite awhile. They are based on 18 concepts originally introduced in the U.K. by Len Masterman. The concepts later migrated to Canada and were shortened to eight. Elizabeth Thoman shortened them to five in the U.S. during the 1990s.

Since 2000, the National Association of Media Literacy Education (NAMLE, formerly AMLA) has defined *media literacy* as empowering:

> Media literacy empowers people to be both critical thinkers and creative producers of an increasingly wide range of messages using image, language, and sound. It is the skillful application of literacy skills to media and technology messages. As communication technologies transform society, they impact our understanding of ourselves, our communities, and our diverse cultures, making media literacy an essential life skill for the 21st century. (http:// namle.net/publications/media-literacy-definitions)

In 2003, the National Board of Professional Teaching Standards (*Adolescence and and Young Adulthood, English Language Arts Standards*) recognized the importance of media and visual literacy when it declared:

Accomplished teachers know that students must become critical and reflective consumers and producers of visual communication because media literacy has become an integral part of being literate in contemporary society. Teachers understand how words, images, graphics, and sounds work together in ways that are both subtle and profound. They understand that students need to learn the power of visual communication, from the uses of typefaces and white space on a written report to the uses of graphics and video in multimedia productions. (NBPTS, 2003, p. 15)

In 2005, the phrases "new literacies" and "21st century literacy" began to become popular. New Media Consortium (NMC) defined this literacy "subset":

[The] abilities and skills where aural, visual, and digital literacy overlap. … These include the ability to understand the power of images and sounds, to recognize and use that power, to manipulate and transform digital media, to distribute them pervasively, and to easily adapt them to new forms. (NMC, 2005, p. 2; http://archive.nmc.org/summit/)

In 2006, the College Board's Standards for College Success in English Language Arts/Media Literacy said:

To be successful in college and in the workplace and to participate effectively in a global society, students are expected to understand the nature of media; to interpret, analyze, and evaluate the media messages they encounter daily; and to create media that express a point of view and influence others. These skills are relevant to all subject areas, where students may be asked to evaluate media coverage of research, trends, and issues. (College Board, p. 171)

In 2009 the annual K–12 *Horizon Report* declared the number one critical challenge for schools as: "a growing need for formal instruction in key new skills, including information literacy, visual literacy, and technological literacy" (Johnson, Levine, & Smith, 2009, para. 2).

The 2010 K–12 *Horizon Report* continued to include this critical challenge when it stated: "Digital media literacy continues its rise in importance as a key skill in every discipline and profession" (Johnson, Levine, Smith, & Stone, 2010, para. 2).

Does Media Literacy Work?

In 2005, the Center for Media Literacy partnered with the Los Angeles Unified School District on an elementary media literacy in the arts program called Project SMARTart. Teachers were introduced to the CML core concepts, and students were engaged in activities that "explored the way ideas are communicated: how to recognize, interpret and convey messages" (Jolls & Grande, 2005, p. 29).

Project SMARTart provided the first formal study of how media literacy can be successfully integrated into an existing school's arts classroom. Two media researchers conducted studies with students in an attempt to fill a void in media literacy education research. Working with high school students in one study and college students in another, the researchers provided solid evidence about the efficacy of media literacy instruction.

In another study, Renee Hobbs and her team worked with a group of high school English educators in Massachusetts. Her work and study are both described in her book, *Reading the Media in High School: Media Literacy in High School English*. She reports that one of the main advantages of teaching media literacy was that students' knowledge of comprehension, analysis, listening, and viewing transferred from non-print to print. Hobbs said:

> … over all, students had a more sophisticated understanding of how authors compose messages to convey meaning through their use of language, image and sound and how readers respond with their own meaning-making processes as they interpret messages. (Hobbs, 2007, p. 148)

Paul Mihailidis, an assistant professor of media studies at Hofstra University, conducted a study of 239 University of Maryland undergraduates. He found that the students enrolled in a media literacy course increased their ability to comprehend, evaluate, and analyze media messages in print, video, and audio formats. The study, published in the *International Journal of Learning and Media*, suggests that media literacy curricula and readings that are solely or primarily focused on teaching critical analysis skills are an essential first step in teaching media literacy (Mihailidis, 2009).

Getting Started

Purchasing pre-produced media literacy curriculum or workbooks might sound like a good idea, but in reality engaging students with real media texts is best. Many educators have found success by starting this way. In most of our schools, we already have access to videos, magazines, newspapers, and films. These can and should be put to use, as you will see, as perfect media literacy curriculum materials. Over the past 15 years, I have developed my own approach to teaching media literacy, beginning with visual literacy, moving to advertising, and then into moving images.

Visual literacy → Advertising → Moving images

I believe students of media first need to understand how images are created and how we interpret and understand the process of reading an image (visual literacy); afterward we can move on to images and words combined, for example, in advertising. Last, students can be introduced to the language of moving images (TV, film, video) and can begin to appreciate the techniques used by producers. We should begin teaching media literacy by starting with the static visual image: that might be a picture in a children's book, a photograph from the news, or a chart/diagram/graphic in a textbook. Known as "visual literacy," this involves learning how to "read" an image in its context and understanding both how it was created and how it is being used. During this first stage, students should also have the opportunity to use cameras to create images. Their images could become part of their homework or simply part of a photographic display. After students learn the language of the image, I believe they will be ready to study images and words together—for example, in an advertisement.

There are literally hundreds of magazines available, and each targets a specific audience. Using a one- or two-page print ad in the classroom is another way to engage students and meet standards at the same time. But ads are not confined to print: they pass our radar screens as billboards, signs on trucks, commercials, product placements in television and film, and more. Once students begin to "read," "analyze," and "deconstruct" these ads, they will be ready to produce some of their own.

Eventually students will certainly be engaged in studying moving images. The phrase "moving images" refers to both television and film. Here, students begin to study genre, narrative, symbolism, representation, production, editing, the languages of TV and film, and much, much more. It is at this stage that students begin collaborating as a team to create scripts and storyboards—important steps in the media-making process. Popular culture also offers teachers a multitude of ideas, programs, and films from which to choose.

Beginning Vocabulary

A number of key words and phrases are part of media literacy education. (Before I owned a mobile phone, I didn't understand what "roaming" meant.) Remember CML's second core concept: "Media messages are constructed using a creative language with its own rules." Because every medium has its own language (words and phrases), it will be important for you and your students to understand what each of these means as they begin to study media literacy. Refer to the glossary in the back of this book for a list of terms and their definitions.

Media Literacy Resources

Websites

Questioning the Media: A Guide for Students (Buckingham, D., 2003, UNESCO)
www.amarc.org/documents/articles/buckingham_guide.pdf

A Guide to Effective Literacy Instruction, Grades 4 to 6
(Ontario Ministry of Education, 2008)
www.media-literacy.ca/welcome/Ideas/
Entries/2008/5/14_Media_Lit._Document_from_the__Ministry_of_Ed._.html

Center for Media Literacy Media Lit Kit
www.medialit.org/bp_mlk.html

Media Awareness Network (Canada)
www.media-awareness.ca

Media Literacy Online Project
http://mlop.proscenia.net

Media Literacy Clearinghouse
www.frankwbaker.com

Books

Introduction to Media Literacy
Moses, L. (Kendall/Hunt, 2010)

Lesson Plans for Creating Media-Rich Classrooms
Christel, M. T., & Sullivan, S., Editors. (National Council of Teachers of English, 2007)

Mass Media and Popular Culture
Duncan, B., D'ippolito, J., Macpherson, C., & Wilson, W. (Harcourt Brace, 1996)

Media Literacy: Keys to Interpreting Media Messages **(3rd edition)**
Silverblatt, A. (Praeger, 2007)

Media Literacy Resource Guide
(Ontario Ministry of Education, 1989)

Persuasion in the Media Age with PowerWeb **(2nd edition)**
Borchers, T. A. (McGraw-Hill, 2004)

Visual Messages: Integrating Imagery into Instruction **(2nd edition)**
Considine, D. M., & Haley, G. E. (Libraries Unlimited, 1999)

Journals

Journal of Media Literacy
http://journalofmedialiteracy.org

Journal of Media Literacy Education
http://namle.net/publications/journal-of-media-literacy-education/

CHAPTER 3

VISUAL LITERACY

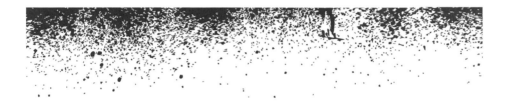

We are a visually illiterate society. ... Three R's are no longer enough. Our world is changing fast—faster than we can keep up with our historical modes of thinking and communicating. Visual literacy—the ability to both read and write visual information; the ability to learn visually; to think and solve problems in the visual domain—will, as the information revolution evolves, become a requirement for success in business and in life.

—Dave Gray, founder of visual thinking company XPLANE

Visual Literacy = Reading Pictures

Visual literacy has been defined as the "ability to understand, interpret and evaluate visual messages" (Bristor & Drake, 1994). According to Wikipedia (2011), "Visual literacy is based on the idea that pictures can be 'read' and that meaning can be communicated through a process of reading."

In 1935, photographer Dorothea Lange, while working for the administration of President Franklin D. Roosevelt, snapped a picture of a migrant farm worker and her starving children at a farm in California where the workers were picking peas. Lange was one of a number of photographers who were hired to document conditions of people during the Great Depression. Little did she know that the photo of Florence Owens, known as "Migrant Mother," and the accompanying news coverage would cause the government to rush food aid to the starving workers.

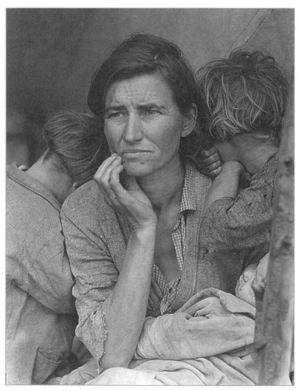

FIGURE 3.1 "Migrant Mother" by Dorothea Lange.

You can read about all of the images Lange took that day at www.loc.gov/rr/print/list/128_migm.html and at www.eyewitnesstohistory.com/migrantmother.htm. A good deconstruction/analysis of the "Migrant Mother" photograph can be found at http://artsedge.kennedy-center.org/educators/lessons/grade-6-8/Migrant_Workers.aspx.

In 1945, when America was still involved in WWII, Ansel Adams photographed Mount Williamson, part of the Sierra Nevada Mountain range in California (Figure 3.2). It is a beautiful image: clouds sit atop the mountain range, and the sun's rays find their way through the clouds, past the mountain to the ground below. In the foreground, large rocks can be seen. It's a nicely balanced photo and represents one of the best landscape photos ever taken. But, might something else be going on here? Media literacy asks us to consider what is outside the frame; what do we not know?

Unless you have studied Adams and his images, you would not have known that this vista was the view for the Japanese-Americans who were detained during World War II in an internment camp located at Manzanar, California. The internees were

FIGURE 3.2 Ansel Adams' photograph of Mount Williamson. Copyright held by the Ansel Adams Publishing Rights Trust.

allowed outside only to collect smaller rocks for their gardens. Now that you know this, does it change the way you understand or feel about the photograph?

For further discussion of this photo, check out Ansel Adams and Japanese Internment Camp Photos (http://memory.loc.gov/ammem/collections/anseladams). Some other photos worthy of discussion can be found at 35 Powerful Photos That Tell a Story (www.noupe.com/photography/35-powerful-photos-that-each-tells-a-story.html).

The first 10 minutes of the 2008 animated feature film *WALL-E* contain no dialogue. There are no words to describe the action; the audience has to interpret what is happening simply by watching and listening to the action on the screen. The action: we meet WALL-E, the garbage-collecting robot whose sole job is to clean up Earth after it has been abandoned by all humans. See a PowerPoint presentation (www.rickinstrell.co.uk/TeachingWallE.ppt) for more information on how *WALL-E* communicates to its audience.

Visual literacy is something that has been primarily confined to our arts classrooms; in the arts, students learn how to look at a painting and how to read, analyze, and deconstruct the techniques used by the artist. Usually they study and become aware of concepts such as lighting, color, composition, and more. Today, the need for visual literacy has spread to other disciplines. Because so much information is communicated visually, it is more important than ever that our students learn what it means to be visually literate. Those who create visual images (such as photographs) do so with a purpose in mind, using certain techniques. In order to "read" or analyze an image, the audience (our students) must be able to understand the purpose and recognize the techniques. Just like media literacy, visual literacy is about analyzing and creating messages. Images can be used to influence and persuade, so it is incumbent upon educators to learn how to teach with and about images and to help our students understand the language of photography.

Whether they are images in a text or a picture book, news photos in the morning's newspaper, or a digitally altered photo of a fashion model on the cover of a magazine—images are a major part of our world. Most of us now take lots of pictures because our mobile phones include embedded cameras. A recent Pew survey found that 83% of American teens take pictures with their cell phones (Lenhart, Ling, Campbell, & Purcell, 2010). More students are into photography because of its accessibility. The size and affordability of smaller cameras makes incorporating images into instruction easier than ever. There are also a host of photo-sharing websites where we can upload and share our images with others.

Standards for Visual Literacy

McREL Language Arts Viewing Standards

The Mid-Continent Research for Education and Learning Corporation offers a well-respected set of standards and benchmarks for K–12 education (Kendall, 2011). McREL's extensive Language Arts standards and benchmarks (www.mcrel.org/standards-benchmarks) include the following:

Standard 9. Uses viewing skills and strategies to interpret visual media

Level I (Grades K–2)

1. Understands the main idea or message in visual media (e.g., graphics, animation, comic books, television)

Level III (Grades 6–8)

6. Understands how symbols, images, sound, and other conventions are used in visual media (e.g., time lapse in films; set elements that identify a particular time period or culture; short cuts used to construct meaning, such as the scream of brakes and a thud to imply a car crash; sound and image used together; the use of close-ups to convey drama or intimacy; the use of long camera shots to establish setting; sequences or groups of images that emphasize specific meaning, differences between visual and print media)

Level IV (Grades 9–12)

7. Understands how images and sound convey messages in visual media (e.g., special effects, camera angles, symbols, color, line, texture, shape, headlines, photographs, reaction shots, sequencing of images, sound effects, music, dialogue, narrative, lighting)

Source: Selected standards reprinted by permission of McREL from *Content Knowledge: A Compendium of Standards and Benchmarks for K–12 Education*.

Continued

Standards for Visual Literacy *(Continued)*

NCTE/IRA Standards for the English Language Arts

The National Council of Teachers of English (NCTE/IRA) clearly acknowledges the importance of teaching students to be visually literate. The organization's preface to its standards (www.ncte.org/standards) states:

> Being literate … means being active, critical, and creative users not only of print and spoken language but also of the visual language of film and television, commercial and political advertising, photography, and more. Teaching students how to interpret and create visual texts … is another essential component of the English language arts curriculum. (NCTE/IRA, 1996, p. 5)

Other Relevant Standards

National Standards for Arts Education
www.educationworld.com/standards/national/arts

The Common Core State Standards Initiative
www.corestandards.org/the-standards/english-language-arts-standards

The Kennedy Center's ArtsEdge
http://artsedge.kennedy-center.org/educators/standards.aspx

Understanding How Photographs Communicate

Here are a few of the techniques and strategies by which a photo conveys meaning:

Angle: The vantage point or direction from which the artist photographs the subject.

Framing: By deciding where the edges of the image will be, the photograph determines what you will (and will not) see—whether the subject will fill the frame and appear "close up" or will be seen at a distance as part of a larger context.

Light: Light is one of the most powerful tools of the photographer. The manipulation of light and dark and the sharpness of contrast between light and dark contribute to the mood a photograph conveys.

Focus: The clarity or blurriness of the image. The range between the nearest and farthest things that appear in clear focus defines the photograph's depth of field.

Composition: What is in the foreground? Are the elements arranged in any particular pattern? Do you see any geometric shapes? Are the lines of the photograph straight or curving, thick or thin? Do any visual elements repeat? Is the visual weight of the photograph balanced: on each side? top to bottom? diagonally? (Adapted from Susan Schekel, personal communication, Stony Brook University)

Using Photographs in the Classroom

For many years, I have been a fan of the news photo awards given annually by *Editor & Publisher* magazine. Each year, newspapers and magazines are recognized for excellence in photography. Categories include hard news, soft news (feature), sports, and more. You can search previous years' winners at www.editorandpublisher.com.

When working with groups of students, I recommend printing out and distributing a different photo to each group. Because they will not likely have had any prior experience analyzing photos, they will need some guidance. I have found the simple Photo Analysis Worksheet (Worksheet 3.1) developed by the National Archives to be particularly useful.

Photo Analysis Worksheet

Step 1. Observation

A. Study the photograph for two minutes. Form an overall impression of the photograph and then examine individual items. Next, divide the photo into quadrants and study each section to see what new details become visible.

B. Use the chart below to list people, objects, and activities in the photograph.

People	Objects	Activities

Step 2. Inference

Based on what you have observed above, list three things you might infer from this photograph.

Step 3. Questions

A. What questions does this photograph raise in your mind?

B. Where could you find answers to them?

WORKSHEET 3.1 Analysis Worksheet: Photograph.

Source: www.archives.gov/education/lessons/worksheets/photo.html also in PDF format: www.archives.gov/education/lessons/worksheets/

Getting Started

Before using the photo analysis handout, it might be helpful to ask the question: What do you see? Students, working in groups, should create a list. I suggest images be used without accompanying captions. (One idea is to cover the photo caption with a piece of construction paper, so that the caption can be read at a later time.) Captions draw students' attention away from the photo, even though they do provide the context. But that is not the goal here. We want students simply to gather information solely from the image itself. When they don't have any context, they are required to look deeply at the photo—and through this process, they will see details they would not have seen otherwise.

After the teacher gives them time to study their photos, representatives of each group should be called on to explain what they observed. (It may be helpful for students to stand in front of the class and hold up their group's photo or for a teacher to project it in the front of the room so that the entire class can see it). After each group has shared its findings, a student should lift the cover from the caption below its photo, and read it aloud. This completes the activity, allowing students to understand the context of the photo.

A host of websites now provide teachers with many options for locating and using photos with students. Here are a few:

Resources for Photos

Daily News Photos
http://news.yahoo.com

> In the "News Search" toolbar on the left, click first on the magnifying glass icon and select the "news photos" option from the drop-down menu. Then enter words that describe what you're searching for to produce a host of images.

The National Archives
www.archives.gov/research/start/by-format.html#photos

***LIFE* Magazine Archives**
http://images.google.com/hosted/life

EduPic Graphical Resource
www.edupic.net

Smithsonian Photography Initiative
http://photography.si.edu

Picturing Modern America 1880–1920
http://cct2.edc.org/PMA/

Read Write Web
www.readwriteweb.com/archives/digital_image_resources_on_the_deep_web.
php

Pictures of the Year International
www.poyi.org/65/winners.html

Pulitzer Prize Winning Photographs
www.pulitzer.org/bycat

Framing

Imagine holding a camera and looking through its viewfinder. You might move the camera, or yourself, in order to improve the composition of the picture inside your viewfinder, and thus your final picture. You are deciding what to include and what to leave out. This is called *framing*. When many of us look at a photograph, we usually don't ask the critical-thinking question: What is outside the frame? But we should. Consider the baby photo examples Debbie Abilock presents on pages 109 and 110 of her NoodleTools "Visual Literacy" handout (see Figures 3.3a and 3.3b; www.noodletools.com/debbie/literacies/visual/diglitnews.pdf).

Check out the news photography framing exercise "How Framing Affects Our Understanding" at www.frankwbaker.com/framing.htm.

FIGURE 3.3a It looks like the baby is reading the newspaper. Its hand is holding the corner of the page, perhaps ready to turn the page, but let's consider what we don't see.

FIGURE 3.3b Now we see the baby is actually sitting on someone's lap. Seeing what's "outside the frame" changes the viewer's understanding.

Visual Literacy Inquiry

Graphic designer Erin Riesland (2005) suggests that students who are learning to incorporate visual literacy into their thinking consider the following questions:

- What am I looking at?

- What does this image mean to me?

- What is the relationship between the image and the displayed text message?

- How is this message effective? (Riesland, 2005, para. 10)

Manipulation of Images

Pick up a magazine aimed at women and, even though it's hard to tell, most likely the cover has been retouched or digitally altered. The use of software programs to change photographic images has become so commonplace that many of us don't realize or recognize it. *Newsweek* magazine has an online gallery worthy of student attention. "Unattainable Beauty," which can be found at www.newsweek.com/feature/2010/unattainable-beauty.html, takes a look at a decade's worth of what it says are bad digital photo alterations and provides background on how the original images were changed.

Another take on this topic that is appropriate for young women is from Sweden. It invites students to discover how magazine covers are manipulated (http://demo. fb.se/e/girlpower/retouch).

Activity

Students can be encouraged to take sides on this issue. Should photographs of models or actors be digitally altered? Have your students conduct their own research. What rights do famous people give up when their photos are used on magazine covers? Do you think retouched images should be labeled with a symbol?

We think of the manipulation of images as a contemporary issue, especially with the advent of Photoshop and other photo-altering software. But the truth is that images have been manipulated since photography was first invented. Examples of this can be seen by going to the website gajitz.com and searching for the article "Before Photoshop: 7 Photo Edits That Literally Made History" (http://gajitz. com/before-photoshop-7-photo-edits-that-literally-made-history).

I've created a lesson plan, "Critically Viewing Photographs," designed to get students thinking about a famous photograph taken after the Battle of Gettysburg. The lesson plan can be found at www. frankwbaker.com/civilwarlessonplan.htm.

Kate Doesn't Like Photoshop

In 2003, actress Kate Winslet made news not for a movie she made but for her comments about how she was portrayed on a magazine cover. The British edition of *Gentleman's Quarterly* magazine featured Winslet, whose legs had been significantly trimmed and tummy flattened. She protested, "The retouching is excessive. I do not look like that and more importantly I don't desire to look like that." In 2005, she objected to photo retouching in a movie poster (Schewe, 2005).

Using New Media Tools With Visual Literacy

A variety of new media tools are now available that allow you and your students to add text within the body of a photograph or image. For example, in my lesson plan about the Civil War photo (www.frankwbaker.com/civilwarlessonplan.htm), I posted a number of questions that can be used as prompts for student discussion. Using user-friendly applications such as Bubble Snaps (www.bubblesnaps.com) or Flickr Notes (as in the example shown at www.flickr.com/photos/caterina/31244/), such questions or comments could be posted inside the photo itself.

Is Seeing Believing?

In 2002, I received an email with the subject line "*National Geographic* 2002 Photo of the Year." Upon opening the email, I was presented with a color photo of what appeared to be a shark coming out of the water about to attack a man coming down the ladder of a helicopter hovering over the water. Wow, I thought, this is impressive, and I forwarded the email to friends.

FIGURE 3.4 A well-done hoax circulated through email.

Source: Unknown.

When I first received the email, I admit, my critical faculties were dropped. It was certainly possible, I reasoned, that *National Geographic*, with photographers literally all over the world, captured this photo of a man about to be attacked by a shark.

Unfortunately, this "photo" does not represent what really happened: it is a digital manipulation. Shortly after the viral email made the rounds, the *National Geographic* website debunked the doctored image (Danielson & Braun, 2005). In explaining the hoax photo, they describe the original two images that were morphed to create the final image.

Students could use the critical-thinking questions and apply them to this image. *Who created the image?* Because it was a viral email, it had no traceable author. All photographers want credit for their work, so when a photo has no caption or author, we should be wary. *What is the purpose of the image?* It is clear that the author/ creator hoped readers would forward it, without question, which many of us did. *Who is the audience for this message?* Anyone who reads email. *What techniques were used to create it?* The author/creator located real images online, used some kind of photo-editing software, and wrote an email that sounded authentic. To check if an email or image is an "urban legend," use the Snopes.com website (www.snopes. com), which researches and reports whether a message is true or false. The Internet shark attack hoax is debunked at www.snopes.com/photos/animals/shark.asp.

Visual Literacy and News Content (News Literacy)

Kate Brigham's thesis, "Decoding Visual News Content" (2002; http://katebrigham. com/thesis/forMIT/Interface.htm) is a valuable resource designed to educate news consumers about the design of news graphics on television and layout in news magazines. The intention of the activities on the site, according to the author, "is to introduce people to some methods for looking more critically at visual news content." She uses the news media coverage about the September 11, 2001, attacks in New York to explore issues. By clicking on Television Stills (for example), you can change the background image or colors. Readers can also explore reasons behind certain image uses, text, visual features, and concepts, as well as explanations of the medium used and the sources of the images.

Visual Literacy in the Political Arena

The next time you see President Obama's photo in the news, remember this: Everything about that image likely will have been carefully thought out ahead of time. Not many people know that the White House has a Communications Department, composed of television and advertising experts, whose sole job it is to make the president look his best in tomorrow's news.

FIGURE 3.5 Indiana Town Hall meeting, February 9, 2009.

Source: White House Photo Blog, www.whitehouse.gov/blog_post/indiana

Yes, a stage will have been built, and a lot of thought goes into what is behind the chief executive. In other words, framing: what the camera sees. The photographers will all be told where to stand to get the "best shot," which is what you will see in the evening news, the morning newspaper, and the weekly news magazine. Image is more important than words; our brains will retain the impressions more than what is said, so image control is paramount. From Abraham Lincoln to Barack Obama, the people in office or running for office have been concerned about their image.

Their aides fret over the question: What do we want the public and the media to see? Their campaign aides and consultants try to control how the media convey the politician's image in the press. "Photo ops" (short for photo opportunities) abound: specific events and times when news photographers can capture the candidates doing anything, from kissing babies to eating lunch. All candidates are interested in how they are represented. Candidates, for example, may wear a coat and tie in order to communicate a serious business or formal message. Or they may dress down, as John Edwards did, wearing blue jeans and no tie for much of his 2008 poverty tour. Or they might wear the color red, as Hillary Clinton did, perhaps to communicate patriotism. Or they may be seated aboard a tank, as Democratic presidential nominee Michael Dukakis did, trying to communicate his strength on America's defense. President G. W. Bush wanted to send a message of a strong leader when he appeared on an aircraft carrier to declare "Mission Accomplished" in Iraq.

Questioning Photographs

How we interpret photographs depends on a number of factors. For example, have you had any photography training that would help you understand framing, composition, depth of field, focus, backlighting, and the like? Have you been exposed to any visual literacy education designed to help you read photographic images? Assuming the answer is no, then you would not necessarily have the skills needed to read the language of photographic images. Professional photographers and photojournalists, who have had training, understand how to use the tools of their trade. They also know how to communicate a message to the audience using those tools. Today, those tools include the ability to capture an event, digitally alter an image, and transmit it thousands of miles in a few minutes. But that wasn't always the case.

FIGURE 3.6 Democratic presidential hopeful Senator Robert Kennedy walking alongside his wife, Ethel, on a beach in Astoria, Oregon. The photo was taken May 28, 1968, just a few days before the Oregon primary.

Source: Photo courtesy of John F. Kennedy Presidential Library, Burton Berinksy.

When thinking about the image of the Kennedys (see Figure 3.6) and what it might represent, we might say that it could be representative of a romantic moment: two people sharing some quiet time, relaxing and alone. The fog in the distance also lends to the mood. We might speculate as to the weather, because the Senator has his hands in his pockets; his wife is wearing a coat. She has taken her shoes off in order to walk in the sand. There appear to be tire tracks in the sand, indicative of a car or some other vehicle having driven there.

How did the photographer know they would be on the beach at that time? Did the Kennedy campaign issue a press release notifying the media that the candidate would be available for a photo op? What was the campaign hoping this image would communicate to voters?

The important thing to remember here is that the Kennedys were not alone. There was a photographer who took this picture; he was situated behind them. His framing of this shot, or the cropping of it, is such that we are not allowed to see what might be to the left or right of the Kennedys. We should ask: what is outside the photographer's viewfinder? What are we not allowed to see and why?

Notice the number of people who can be seen in the wider shot (Figure 3.7). How do you feel about the first photograph, now that you've seen the second one? Does this change your impression or your understanding of this staged event? We might ask, who are those people surrounding the candidate and his wife?

FIGURE 3.7 A subsequent image of Robert and Ethel Kennedy taken by the same photographer a short time later.

Source: Photo courtesy of John F. Kennedy Presidential Library, Burton Berinksy.

Contemporary Use of Images for Political Purposes

In the winter of 2010, President Barack Obama was on a campaign to win support of his health care legislation. One event at the White House was covered by the news media, and photographs of it were published in newspapers, magazines, blogs, and other news-related web pages.

FIGURE 3.8 U.S. President Barack Obama speaking about his health care proposals.

Source: Associated Press photo by Susan Walsh, October 5, 2009.

The photo shows the president speaking from a podium, flanked by people wearing white coats. Thinking about visual literacy, we might ask students to consider the following questions: Who are the people surrounding the president? Did you say doctors? If so, how do you know? If they are doctors, did they arrive at the White House wearing these coats? Is it possible that the White House distributed the coats to them? Why would it be necessary or desirable for the President to be photographed with "doctors" in white coats? What might this image communicate to news consumers?

For more material on how politicians use images, visit The People's Choice: Digital Imagery and the Art of Persuasion (Burns & Martinez, 2002), at http://web.archive.org/web/20040105032819/www.southcentralrtec.org/alt/files/people%27schoice/17+Art+of+Persuasion.pdf. This professional development module (with lesson plans and resources) teaches about visual literacy with a focus on past presidential campaigns' visual messages.

Reading a Magazine Cover

Magazine covers are like advertisements. The graphic designers put the most controversial content on the cover in order to capture our attention and get us to purchase it. Students should be encouraged to read a cover.

The editors and designers of the *Rolling Stone* example shown in Figure 3.9 placed a caricature of President Bush on the cover of an issue when he was the chief executive. In order to read this cover, you must be able to interpret some of what is portrayed. For example, would students know that Bush is

FIGURE 3.9 The May 4, 2006, *Rolling Stone* cover.

Art: Robert Grossman

wearing a "dunce cap"? Would they know the meaning of it? Would they also understand what it means to be "sitting in the corner of the room"? Ask students to "read" or decipher the expression on the face of the president. What might it mean or convey? Because many teachers also teach bias, what might we have our students infer from the *Rolling Stone* editors' use of the caricature, combined with the words "The Worst President in History"?

FIGURE 3.10 The December 8, 2008, cover of the *New Yorker* magazine.

Examine the cover of the *New Yorker* magazine shown in Figure 3.10. In order to read/understand this cover, you must know what was happening in the news during this time. For context, Senator Barrack Obama had just been elected President of the United States in November. It would also be necessary to understand that all incoming presidents must interview and select key members of their staff. What else was in the news? Senator Obama's two daughters were promised they would get a new dog when they moved into the White House.

Using the above background information, what might you infer is happening on the magazine cover?

Magazine Covers as Symbolic Representations

Those who design the covers of magazines also communicate to readers using symbolism. Take a look at the magazine covers shown in Figure 3.11. Ask students to deconstruct these covers and explain their symbolism. What are the graphic designers and editors trying to communicate?

FIGURE 3.11 Magazine covers for students to deconstruct.

Activities

Check out the magazine deconstruction activity from the Center for Media Literacy at http://web.archive.org/web/20041024154540/http://www.medialit.org/pdf/CML_DeconstructionMags.pdf). There you will find two magazine covers of former California Governor Arnold Schwarzenegger to compare and contrast. Another good example for comparing and contrasting are the two magazine covers (see Figure 3.12) featuring NBA athlete LeBron James.

Have students consider these questions:

- Who are the audiences for each magazine?

- What are the clues?

- What are one or two adjectives that could describe how LeBron looks on each cover?

FIGURE 3.12 LeBron James on two magazine covers.

Magazine covers are also ads. What techniques are used to sell magazines to their readers? Notice LeBron's facial expressions: what do they say to you? If you could read only one of these publications (*Sports Ilustrated* or *GQ*), which would it be, and why? In other words, which is more appealing? If you were to re-design each cover, what would you change, and why?

Sample Magazine Cover Deconstruction

In the following example, students would have to understand certain terms, such as "masthead" (the title of a newspaper or periodical as it appears across the first page), to comprehend this analysis. Explanations of this magazine cover, from the United Kingdom, are posted on the Magforum website (www.magforum.com/cover_secrets.htm) and under Gender/Magazine Covers and Cover Lines at www.katpad.co.uk/media08/page6.html.

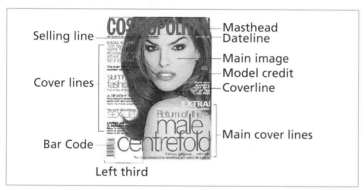

FIGURE 3.13 The secrets of magazine cover design (www.magforum.com/cover_secrets.htm).

Have students bring in a favorite magazine. Introduce them to some of the elements of "informational texts," for example: layout, cover line, vanishing line, selling line, heading/subhead, sidebar, and balance.

Direct them to create an analysis or deconstruction of their magazine covers (refer to Worksheet 3.2).

Informational Text Questions Worksheet
(Note: Not all of the questions would apply to every text.)

1. Who is the author of this text, and who is the publisher?

2. What is the purpose of the text? What does the author/publisher hope to gain by creating it?

3. Does the text indicate any bias or propaganda techniques? If so, identify them.

4. Which text features stand out?

5. Could the text be described as a primary or secondary source?

6. Who is the intended audience; what does the creator hope the audience will do?

7. What is appealing in the text?

8. How are headlines, colors, and font styles and sizes used?

9. Could this text have been presented in a different form? If so, what form?

10. Create a few words or phrases that describe this text.

WORKSHEET 3.2 Informational Text Questions Worksheet.

Source: www.frankwbaker.com

Students could post their productions on a class blog or via sites such as SlideShare. net. Students analyzing the same magazine or perhaps the same cover subject on different magazines might also compare and contrast their analyses.

See how a student created his own magazine cover at http://georgiamedia.wordpress. com/2010/02/22/productio-log-220210. Have your students create their own magazine covers. Just Google the phrase "create a magazine cover," and you will find a number of websites that will allow your students to produce their own covers. They might also prefer to create a parody of a magazine cover.

See Figure 3.14 for an example of a "fake" *National Geographic* magazine cover created by the *Harvard Lampoon*. Have students compare this fake cover with an authentic *National Geographic* cover. What text and visual features are alike; which ones are different? In what ways might Paris Hilton be a "wild animal"?

FIGURE 3.14 The mock *National Geographic* cover of the *Harvard Lampoon*, which appeared April 1, 2008 (http://msnbcmedia.msn.com/j/msnbc/Components/ Photo_StoryLevel/080401/080401-harvard-lampoon- vmed-8a.widec.jpg).

Bogus Websites: Manipulating Images and Words

As students conduct research and look for information online, they will invariably come across something that appears to be authentic but, upon closer examination, analysis, and questioning, they'll discover that someone is out to fool them. They'll find that someone has used specific techniques to make a website, photo, or magazine cover look real—but it is not real.

One example is an ad that ran in a Philadelphia newspaper for the new airliner, "Derrie-Air," which proudly announced that customers could book a seat based solely on their weight. They even created a website, http://flyderrie-air.com (see Figure 3.15), which newspaper readers clicked on. Here is what the website looks like: A big practical joke, it seems. The airline does not exist, but many unsuspecting news consumers were taken in by this parody.

FIGURE 3.15 A fake website for a fake airline.

FIGURE 3.16 An advertisement for the made-up drug HAVIDOL.

Another fake ad was done by Australian artist Justine Cooper for a new prescription drug, HAVIDOL (see Figure 3.16). If you're not visually or media literate, you may not think twice about this new drug. Yet this, too, is a parody. Check out the HAVIDOL website, http://havidol.com.

Like the airline ad, the HAVIDOL ad uses certain codes and conventions that we take for granted. Have students consider what made these ads appear to be authentic. What are the clues? For example, every ad touts the product's name and slogan. Have your students identify those. Ask students to consider in what ways these ads resemble the real (airline and prescription drug) ads they are based on.

Read More About It

Read more about the Derrie-Air ad hoax here: www.citytv.com/toronto/citynews/life/money/article/2419--phony-airline-website-comes-too-close-to-reality.

Read more about the background of the fake HAVIDOL ad at www.reuters.com/article/idUSL165119520070216.

Editorial Cartoons in the Social Studies Classroom

One of the best ways to engage students in visual and news literacy is by incorporating editorial cartoons in the classroom. Because editorial cartoons are traditionally found in newspapers and magazines, they are easily accessible. With Internet access, teachers and students can locate cartoons from every newspaper in the U.S., as well as those from all over the world. A number of good cartoon indexes exist, including those in the following list. Note that both Daryl Cagle websites (www.cagle.com and www.cagle.com/teacher) have worksheets, lesson plans, editorial cartoons, and more.

Resources for Cartoon Indexes

Daryl Cagle's Professional Cartoonists Index
www.cagle.com and www.cagle.com/teacher

The Association of American Editorial Cartoonists
http://editorialcartoonists.com

GoComics
www.gocomics.com/explore/editorials

Daryl Cagle's Political Cartoons
www.politicalcartoons.com

Cartoon Stock
www.cartoonstock.com/newscartoons/newscartoon.asp

Questioning Cartoons

Daryl Cagle (Taylor, 2011, para. 6) suggests students use the following five questions to analyze cartoons.

1. What is the event or issue that inspired the cartoon?

2. Are there any real people in the cartoon? Who is portrayed in the cartoon?

3. Are there symbols in the cartoon? What are they and what do they represent?

4. What is the cartoonist's opinion about the topic portrayed in the cartoon?

5. Do you agree or disagree with the cartoonist's opinion? Why? (www.nelrc.org/changeagent/cartoons.htm)

Cartoon Analysis

The National Archives has produced the Cartoon Analysis Worksheet (Worksheet 3.3) to help teachers and students.

The Graphic Novel

Some of the most popular texts in libraries today are graphic novels. Many media specialists report that students can't get enough of these new "comic books." Graphic novels offer many of our students a new avenue to reading by combining words and images in a format that is appealing, attractive, and fun. Reading a graphic novel may seem like a waste of time to some; in reality, as Allyson Lyga (2006) points out, graphic novels offer another way to teach students literacy:

> To read a graphic novel, much less a wordless one, many essential literacy skills are required, including the ability to understand a sequence of events, interpret characters' nonverbal gestures, discern the story's plot, and make inferences. (Lyga, 2006, para. 4)

I have been fascinated not only by the traditional graphic novels based on classic literature, but also by newer trends in nonfiction graphic novels. For example, *The 9-11 Report: A Graphic Adaptation*, illustrated by Sid Jacobson and Ernie Colon (2006), was endorsed by the official 9-11 Commission, and *08: A Graphic Diary of the Campaign Trail*, by Michael Crowley and Dan Goldman, follows both Senators John McCain and Barack Obama on the road to the White House.

Cartoon Analysis Worksheet

Level 1

Visuals	Words (not all cartoons include words)
List the objects or people you see in the cartoon.	Identify the cartoon caption and/or title. Locate three words or phrases used by the cartoonist to identify objects or people within the cartoon. Record any important dates or numbers that appear in the cartoon.

Level 2

Visuals	Words
Which of the objects on your list are symbols? What do you think each symbol means?	Which words or phrases in the cartoon appear to be the most significant? Why do you think so? List adjectives that describe the emotions portrayed in the cartoon.

Level 3

Describe the action taking place in the cartoon.

Explain how the words in the cartoon clarify the symbols.

Explain the message of the cartoon.

What special interest groups would agree/disagree with the cartoon's message?

Why?

WORKSHEET 3.3 Analysis Worksheet: Cartoon.

Source: www.archives.gov/education/lessons/worksheets/cartoon.html also in PDF format:
www.archives.gov/education/lessons/worksheets/

There is even a graphic novel about media literacy. *Media Meltdown: A Graphic Guide Adventure,* written by Liam O'Donnell and illustrated by Mike Deas, is one of the first graphic novels to address media literacy. It's an engaging story of what happens when young people get involved in their community, try to tell a story, and learn about how the media works along the way. You can read more about this book at the Orca website (http://us.orcabook.com/productdetails.cfm?PC=2304). This book even has its own dedicated website (www.mediameltdown.net).

There are a growing number of graphic novel resources on the Internet. Some, such as Comic Life (http://plasq.com/comiclife), Comiqs (http://comiqs.com/aboutus), Pixton (http://pixton.com), and BitStrips (www.bitstrips.com), offer opportunities for your students to create their own comics or graphic novels.

Other websites offer tips and training for teachers looking to integrate graphic novels into their instruction. The Teaching Resources Center of the University of North Carolina at Greensboro has posted "Getting Started with Graphic Novels: A Selective Bibliography of Professional Resources for Librarians" (www.uncg.edu/soe/trc/docs/GraphicNovelsPro_getting%20_started.pdf), which is a great starting place for librarians and teachers. Drawing Words Writing Pictures (http://dw-wp.com/teaching-resources/) is another excellent teacher site. You'll also want to check out all the titles in Will Eisner's instructional series, including: *Comics and Sequential Art: Principles and Practices from the Legendary Cartoonist; Graphic Storytelling and Visual Narrative;* and *Expressive Anatomy for Comics and Narrative: Principles and Practices from the Legendary Cartoonist.*

Visual Literacy Resources

Websites

Visual Literacy: Media Literacy Clearinghouse
www.frankwbaker.com/vis_lit.htm

Visual Information Literacy: Reading a Documentary Photograph, by Debbie Abilock
http://aasl.metapress.com/content/n58l04h238135346/fulltext.pdf

21st Century Literacies, links
www.noodletools.com/debbie/literacies/

Books

Teaching Visual Literacy in the Primary Classroom **Tim Stafford**
Stafford, T. (Routledge, 2010)

Picture This: Photography Activities for Early Childhood Learning **(2nd ed.)**
Entz, S. (Corwin, 2009)

Engaging the Eye Generation: Visual Literacy Strategies for the K–5 Classroom
Riddle, J. (Stenhouse, 2009)

Visual Impact, Visual Teaching: Using Images to Strengthen Learning **(2nd ed.)**
Gangwer, T. (Corwin, 2009)

Teaching Visual Literacy: Using Comic Books, Graphic Novels, Anime, Cartoons, and More to Develop Comprehension and Thinking Skills
Frey, N., & Fisher, D. (Corwin, 2008)

How to Read a Photograph: Lessons from Master Photographers
Jeffrey, I. (Abrams Books, 2009)

CHAPTER 4

ADVERTISING

If students can learn to analyze the commercials they see on TV, they will be better equipped to evaluate the claims that advertisers make; they will be able to look beyond the sell and become less likely victims of deception; and they will learn to separate the double-talk from the facts.

—Don Kaplan, *Television and the Classroom*

The year is 2054; detective John Anderton is on the run and has just entered a shopping mall. With stores and advertising surrounding him, Anderton is startled to hear one of the ads, from American Express, "speak" to him: "It looks like you need an escape, and Blue can take you there." If this sounds far-fetched, you may be right, but the scene from the 2002 film *Minority Report* is based on what futurists predict will happen; it's called "product placement" or "target marketing," and in some ways it's already in use today (see, for example, the website Product Placement News at http://productplacement.biz).

American Express was just one of about a dozen product placements in *Minority Report*. Director Steven Spielberg's intention was to use real advertisers for this "future-reality film." Incidentally, product placement deals bolstered the film's earnings by millions of dollars (Friedman, 2002).

If there is one topic that meets many of the goals and objectives of media literacy, it is advertising. Advertising can be found in so many locations and formats that it is hard to ignore. Advertising also influences its audiences—why else would so many companies advertise if it didn't work? The purpose of advertising is clear: it wants to convince us to buy something. But there are other purposes as well. Advertising wants to get our attention, make us remember, and make an impact—it wants to create an emotional connection—so that we won't forget the product, candidate, issue, or service.

It's Up to the Audience

Advertising also makes promises, but it is up to the audience to decide if the promises hold up. For example, a toothpaste ad might promise not only whiter teeth, but also better relationships. Do you think this is true? Why does advertising exist? Because many of us are not ad experts, we may not be aware that advertising helps pay for much of the media we enjoy. For example, "American Idol" would not be broadcast by the FOX TV network if the producers had not first secured enough advertisers to purchase time during the reality show. That's right: if it weren't for the advertisers, many mass media would simply disappear.

Many Internet sites and most newspapers and magazines depend on advertisers, too. Another thing most students should understand is that advertising is designed to reach a certain demographic or target audience. Sometimes this is referred to as "the eyeballs," (e.g., whose eyeballs does this advertiser want to reach?) A good question for students to consider is Who is the audience for this ad?

The Media Studies website of Benton Park School, Leeds, England, has an excellent section on demographics (www.katpad. co.uk/media08/page9.html) if you'd like to delve a bit deeper into the topic.

Thinking Like Advertisers

When I introduce advertising, I ask my audience to think like advertisers. Imagine that you have a product to sell. You must know who your audience is:

- Who is likely to be interested in this?

- What does the audience know about my product, and what do I want them to know?

- How do I reach them, and what technology or media do they read, listen to, or watch?

- What event or person can I associate with my product? Think celebrity spokesperson or high-profile event, such as the Super Bowl or the Academy Awards.

- What techniques will get their attention (e.g., a blinking ad online; a billboard in a high traffic area)?

- What will it cost me to advertise, and is that purchase cost-effective?

- Can I get my product featured inside the plot of a TV show or movie or on the hood of race car (product placement)?

- What incentives (e.g., a discount coupon) or other techniques can I use to get them to purchase it?

Students, Technology, and Advertisements

"Students in our society are constantly bombarded by advertisements. Technology has not only added to the impact and quantity of advertising but has led to the development and proliferation of new types of advertising. Fortunately, technology is a powerful tool in the hands of students for investigating and understanding the impact of advertising on their lives."

—NETS•S: Connecting Curriculum and Technology (ISTE, 2000, p. 250)

One of the places where studying advertising fits best is in the English language arts, where standards reference the text and visual features of "informational texts." Students can be directed to examine fonts, layout, design, color, and more. Many state's ELA standards also make references to students being able to understand and identify various "techniques of persuasion" or "propaganda techniques." Here are a few of the more common techniques:

Bandwagon: Everyone is doing it; everyone is using it.

Testimonial: I use this product; so should you.

Ordinary/Everyday people: They look like me, and they're using it.

Fear: Something bad may happen if you don't buy this product.

The Media Literacy Project website (www.nmmlp.org/media_literacy/language_persuasion.html) maintains a good list of various persuasion techniques.

Weasel Words in Advertising

Copywriter George Laflin Miller, writing under the pen name Aesop Glim, coined the phrase "weasel words" to mean those vague, overused terms in advertising copy. He got the name from the actual weasel, which literally sucks the life out of eggs it finds. He said that "weasel words" are "undependable words because they describe anything or nothing" (Wright, Winter, Zeigler, & O'Dea, 1982, p. 269).

Jeffrey Schrank, in his widely reprinted essay, "The Language of Advertising Claims" (http://home.olemiss.edu/~egjbp/comp/ad-claims.html), lists some commonly used weasel words, including:

> *helps* (the champion weasel); *like* (used in a comparative sense); *virtual* or *virtually*; *acts* or *works*; *can be*; *up to*; *as much as*; *refreshes*; *comforts*; *tackles*; *fights*; *come on*; *the feel of*; *the look of*; *looks like*; *fortified*; *enriched*; and *strengthened*.

Other "weasely" words include: *best, ideal, better, perfect, extra special, real bargain, superior performance, good, great, top quality, highest quality*, and *variety of uses*. (Wright et al., 1982, p. 269).

Activity

Using a variety of ads from newspapers, magazines, and the web, ask students to locate ads that use weasel words or phrases. Once they've found such ads, categorize the ones that use the same or similar words or phrases. Working in groups, come up with words or phrases that might be better replacements or that clarify exactly what the copywriter might have meant. A good question for students to consider might be: What exactly is the copywriter trying to convey? For example, "Tide works better than the other leading detergent" might be changed to "Tide got the dirt out of 10 soiled shirts, while the other leading brand did not." Have students work together to create or draw the new ad. Post the before and after ads on a bulletin board, blog, or wiki site. There are a number of free (and inexpensive) websites that allow students to create and design their own ads. Do a Google search and determine which one might work best for you and your students. By teaching students how to analyze ads, we are fulfilling ELA Standards.

Advertising in ELA Standards

National Council of Teachers of English/International Reading Association Standards for the English Language Arts

> **NCTE Standard 6.** Students apply knowledge of language structure, language conventions (e.g., spelling and punctuation), media techniques, figurative language, and genre to create, critique, and discuss print and nonprint texts. (NCTE, 1996, p. 26; www.ncte.org/standards, para. 14)

Partnership for 21st Century Skills

> **P21 Information and Media Literacy,** sample student outcome for the 4th grade English standard.
>
> Make a record of commercials aired during Saturday morning cartoon programming. Categorize and tally such details as the kinds of products advertised, the method(s) the ad uses to attract younger viewers, the gender the ad seems to address, and estimated ages of children appearing in the ads. Select several of the ads and survey schoolmates about which ads are favorites. Analyze the survey for patterns of popular appeal. What are "patterns of popular appeal?" (www.p21.org/Matrices/ICTmap_english.pdf, p.1)

Continued

Advertising in ELA Standards *(Continued)*

McREL Language Arts Standards

Standard 9. Uses viewing skills and strategies to interpret visual media

Level II (Grades 3–5)

7. Understands basic elements of advertising in visual media

Level III (Grades 6–8)

4. Understands the use of stereotypes and biases in visual media

8. Knows that people with special interests and expectations are the target audience for particular messages or products in visual media; and knows that design, language, and content reflect this

Level IV (Grades 9–12)

10. Understands a variety of techniques used in advertising

Source: Selected standards reprinted by permission of McREL from *Content Knowledge: A Compendium of Standards and Benchmarks for K–12 Education.*

Elementary Approach

The youngest students can begin to understand advertising by learning about signs. You might ask them, with the help of their parents, to make a list of or draw pictures of all the signs they come in contact with in a day. Students could be introduced to advertising, via signs, by asking them a series of questions, such as: What is a sign? What is the purpose of most signs? Why are some signs located near roads, stores, sports facilities? Why do some signs have words, while others do not? Why are some signs in color, while others are not? Are billboards signs? Are advertisements signs?

A favorite activity of students is to match the product with its advertising slogan. A number of websites provide this kind of information. Be careful, because some of the products (and their slogans) may be too old or advanced for younger students to recognize. Another related activity is the branding alphabet. Most of us have been branded: We can recognize the name of an advertiser based solely on one letter!

Look at Heidi Cody's art in Figure 4.1, which also appears in "The Fine Art of Persuasion: Television & Advertising," one of the class programs offered by The Paley Center for Media (assets.paleycenter.org/assets/education/classPDFs/artpersuasion.pdf, p. 3). See how many product names your students can identify based on one letter.

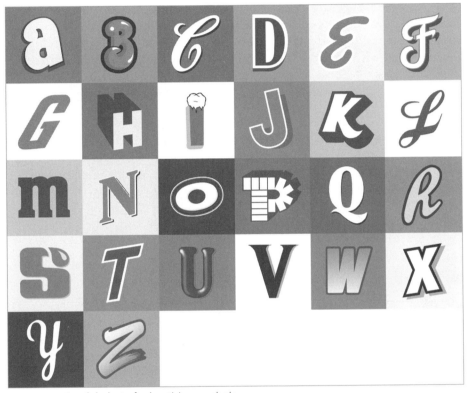

FIGURE 4.1 An alphabet of advertising symbols.

Source: © heidicody.com, reprinted by permission.

Answer Key:

A All	**H** Hebrew National	**O** Oreo	**V** V8
B Bubblicious	**I** ICEE	**P** Pez	**W** Wisk
C Campbell's Soup	**J** Jell-O	**Q** Q-Tip	**X** Xtra
D Dawn	**K** Kool-Aid	**R** Reese's	**Y** York
E Eggo	**L** Lysol	**S** Starburst	Peppermint Pattie
F Frito	**M** M&M's	**T** Tide	**Z** Zest
G Gatorade	**N** Nilla Wafers	**U** Uncle Ben's	

After learning about signs, slogans, and brands, another approach at the elementary level might be the breakfast cereal box. Most students will have seen their favorite cereal already advertised on television, so when they go to the grocery store with a parent, they recognize the name of the cereal, if not the design of the box itself. In what ways are these products persuasive? You might invite them to bring in a favorite cereal box and engage them in a deconstruction activity.

Typical questions at this time might be: What makes this cereal and cereal box appealing? How are colors used to make it attractive? How does the cereal maker use words? What nutritional information, if any, might be promoted? What information might be omitted? What characters or prizes might be portrayed as enticements? After an analysis of the boxes, students might be challenged to create their own boxes using some of the same techniques they've just learned.

One of the critical thinking questions is: Who is the audience for this message? To get students thinking about audience, try this activity: pull several different ads from a variety of magazines. Place the covers of the magazines up on the board and ask students to consider who the target audiences for both the ads and the covers might be. Have students match the ads with the magazine cover from which it originated. Most students have never been taught how to "read" an ad. Once you have introduced the Media Literacy Center's Five Core Concepts and Critical Thinking Questions (www.medialit.org/five-key-questions-can-change-world) to them, they can begin to think critically about how these ads work to inform, influence, and persuade.

I frequently use the pizza ad (see Figure 4.2) with my audiences. A good starting question might be, What do you see? Students working in groups could begin by making a list of every word on the page (even those in the smallest possible font), identifying the slogan(s), the name of product, the name of the advertiser, and listing every image they see.

In this particular ad, a lot is going on; on first read, not all students might comprehend everything that's going on. They should be able to identify the slogan (What you really want!); the name of the product (Tony's Original Crust Pepperoni Pizza); the story (what is going on in the picture: the hang-gliding girl swoops in to steal a slice from the boys' clubhouse); and the name of the parent company for Tony's (turning the ad horizontally, students will find the name Schwann's).

Older students may possibly understand the notion of *subtext*, the underlying or implied messages in the same ad, such as power relationships: Who has more power;

FIGURE 4.2 A Tony's Pizza advertisement (from *Nickelodeon* and *Disney Adventure* magazines).

Color version: www.frankwbaker.com/pizza_ad

who has less? All audiences should consider the colors in the ad (the hang-glider contains the same colors as the pizza package); the eye movement or how your eye moves along the page (arts educators can also help explain the "rule of thirds" and how important elements fall along certain lines); the point of view (POV; we see this action from a high angle); the techniques of persuasion; and what is omitted (such as the price of the pizza and the nutritional information). Students might also use the Donna Ogle's (1986) K-W-L model: What do you Know? What do you Want to know? What have you Learned?

The 5 Ps Approach

Media educator David Considine teaches with and about advertising using the "5 Ps" approach, something he first promoted in his 1999 book, *Visual Messages: Integrating Imagery into Instruction* (coauthored with Gail E. Haley). He suggests teachers create a template that explains the 5 Ps to help students understand how advertising and marketing work.

> **Product:** What product or service is being pitched?

> **Purchasers:** Who is the audience for the pitch?

> **Pitch:** What technique of persuasion is used?

> **Placed or placement:** Where do you find this (magazine, newspaper, TV, film, web)?

> **Presented:** In what form or package? (Considine, 2010, p. 15)

Advertising in a Web 2.0 World

Advertising is everywhere, especially online. Ads can be found on blogs, wikis, Nings, and on our mobile phones. Because each screen is different, ads are being customized for each new medium and technology. Students can compare and contrast how one ad appears across different media platforms. Students should also understand that "search results" can be affected by advertising and marketing, and that their every move online is being tracked by some firm that wants to sell them something.

Many unsuspecting students, already fans of social networking, don't realize that the more they reveal about themselves (location, hobbies, likes, dislikes), the more information they're actually providing to marketing and advertising firms. Privacy begins to fade away. Natasha Singer wrote an article in the *New York Times* (2010) that called attention to this so-called "stealth marketing":

> Cameras that can follow you from the minute you enter a store … Web coupons embedded with bar codes that can identify and alert retailers to the search terms you used … Mobile marketers that can find you near a store clothing rack, and send ads to your cellphone.

Resources for Web 2.0 World

Teaching Advertising with YouTube Videos
www.theadclass.com/education/using-youtube-to-teach-advertising-creativity

A collection of short clips from and about the advertising industry

Advertising Age Magazine
www.adage.com

This weekly magazine makes a good starting point for reading and understanding how advertisers are hoping to reach us through social networks and other digital technologies.

whatis.com site
http://whatis.techtarget.com/definition/0,,sid9_gci211535,00.html

This section of the whatis.com site has an extensive glossary of the advertising terminology used on the Internet.

Using VoiceThread to Teach Advertising Literacy

One of the more interesting uses of VoiceThread software is to get student feedback and reactions to certain ads that target them. For example, in Travis Elementary in Mineral Wells, Texas, sixth grade teacher Dianne Aldridge used VoiceThread to engage her students in an analysis of a print ad for a Nike shoe (see the video "A Little Less Gravity," made in October 2009, at http://travistechies.wikispaces.com/ Media+Literacy+VoiceThread).

On her web page, Aldridge says that her students had no prior experience in ad deconstruction or with using VoiceThread before she began this exercise. She calls VoiceThread a "fabulous tool" that enables her students to reach the highest level of Bloom's Taxonomy for Higher Order Thinking (Bloom, 1956).

At the start of the VoiceThread, we hear and see her ask the question: "I wonder what you think 'a little less gravity' means? Who's the target audience?" Each of the icons, in the columns to the left and right of the ad, represents students who are invited to comment on the question (see Figure 4.3). They can react by typing a response, recording an audio response, or recording a video response. During any of their comment opportunities, they can interact with the ad by using a drawing tool to highlight or circle a portion of the ad.

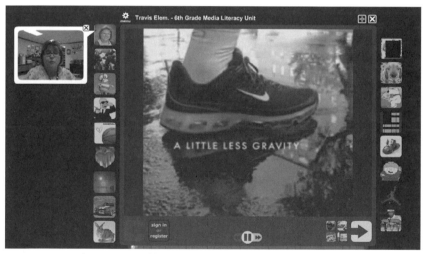

FIGURE 4.3 Teacher Dianne Aldridge's VoiceThread page.

Product Placement

Advertising appears inside our favorite television shows and movies, not just during commercial breaks. Product placement involves a paid transaction, in which an advertiser pays to have a product appear visibly, inside the content of a program or film. Advertisers know that because of digital technology, many in the audience can zap (skip) the commercials. So to get maximum exposure for their products, advertisers have started paying television and film producers to place products *inside* the production.

Modern product placement made news in the 1982 movie *E.T.: The Extra-Terrestrial* when character Elliott used Reese's Pieces candy to attract the alien. Reports said sales of the candy soared. If you watch "American Idol" on television, you may have already recognized the visible Coke cups (see Figure 4.4) on the table in front of the judges.

Some advertisers believe the on-screen placement of their product is more valuable than the traditional 30-second commercial. If that is true, expect to see a lot more product placement in television.

FIGURE 4.4 Fox's "American Idol" prominently features Coke cups on the judges' table.

Activity

Assign students one week to watch TV programs, but instead of paying attention to the commercials, have them track appearances of product placement. Using a stopwatch, they can time how long the product stays on the screen. At the end of the week, they will present their findings. Can students make any conclusions? For example, does one network have more programs with product-placement appearances?

Advertising Formula

Older students should know the acronym AIDA (Strong, 1925) and be able to apply it to various types of ads aimed at different audiences. Copywriters use this attention-interest-desire-action formula to construct their ads:

Attention: The first job of any advertisement is to gain your attention. This might be achieved by the use of bold colors, an interesting image, or an intriguing phrase.

Interest: The ad needs to hold your interest long enough to tell you about its product or service. This might be done, for example, through the use of visual appeal of the ad, asking questions, or creating suspense. Humor or surprise can also grab and hold the audience's interest.

Desire: Positive associations of words and images make the product seem attractive, but readers also need to be convinced that owning the product will improve or enhance their lives. Emotional appeals are commonly used to provoke desire, as in an ad for insurance that urges you to "secure your family's future," which is an appeal to your desire to ensure the security of those closest to you.

Action: The advertisement must prompt the audience to take action and buy the product. Often, this is done through creating a sense of urgency by the use of phrases such as, "Pick up the phone today!' and "Free gift for the first 100 callers." (Breuer & Napthine, 2008, p. 2)

To see some examples of print ads deconstructed using the AIDA formula, check out the Dark Pines: Media Literacy Blog at http://darkpinesmedia.wordpress.com/2010/04/27/media-literacy-aida.

Advertising and Social Studies

NETS•S and Social Studies: You Want to Sell Me What?

ISTE, in collaboration with the U.S. Department of Education, has published a NETS•S social studies lesson plan for Grades 3–5 (2000, pp. 186–190). This lesson plan is also available online: http://web.archive.org/web/20021121023347/http://cnets.iste.org/students/pdf/3-5FormsofAdvertising.pdf.

The "You Want to Sell Me What?" lesson plan encourages students to consider the powerful role that advertising plays in our lives. It is correlated to social studies standards and to the original (2000) National Educational Technology Standards for Students.

The Role of Media In Politics

Candidates who hope to get elected today must get their message out to voters, and television is still their medium of choice. The 30-second commercial has become a staple in American politics.

During the 2008 race for the White House, Barack Obama's first commercial, entitled "The Country I Love," featured the then-senator talking directly to the camera about his qualifications while acoustic guitar music could be heard playing in the background. That night, Jon Stewart made a reference on "The Daily Show" to this spot, telling his audience that anything would sound good with light guitar music playing. Stewart began reading a description of mad cow disease while his band played guitar music. The audience howled with laughter and applause. Stewart had just taught millions of people (his viewing audience) the quintessential media literacy lesson—music can be used to make us feel comfortable, no matter what the subject.

Every four years, we are bombarded by commercials for candidates running for the White House. But local races continue year in and year out and, like the presidential candidates, local politicians employ media consultants who help them craft the right message so that we, the voters, won't forget to vote for them.

Activity

Students can be encouraged to contact local media (radio, TV, newspapers) to determine what their advertising rates are. Taking the role of the media consultant, students, working in groups and representing different candidates, can simulate purchasing ad time in various media in an attempt to reach the widest possible audience.

Techniques in Political Ads

The people who make a candidate's commercials are experts at using imagery and symbolism. In the teaching module "The People's Choice: Digital Imagery and the Art of Persuasion," authors Mary Burns and Danny Martinez (2002) reveal a few tricks and techniques used in these ads, such as the use of complementary colors (red, white, and blue, for example) to promote a sense of patriotism and dressing candidates in certain types of clothing to connote strength, vigor, or authority.

Other techniques include music and sound to provide a certain type of ambience or mood. Superimposed words are used to emphasize the speaker's words. Code words are often used to provoke reflexive, almost visceral, viewer reactions. Props, such as desks, planes, podiums, and other people, are placed to connote action, power, authority, and warmth. Symbols such as children and flags imply patriotism and caring.

Types of Political Ads

In addition to various techniques, political ads also use a variety of types of approaches. The following list comes from a video recording titled *The Classics of Political Television Advertising*.

Profile spots (a biography) are commonly used at the start of a campaign to introduce voters to the candidate.

Testimonial spots feature plain folks or well-known personalities who talk about why they support the candidate.

Accomplishment spots are where the candidate lays out what he/she has already done in office, using memorable visuals.

Negative record spots are where candidates go after each other's record.

Response spots are where the candidate responds to their opponent.

Character challenge spots are often called "mudslinging ads." Challenging your opponent's character can be risky, complex, and delicate.

Issue spots feature candidates talking about issues, even if it is only for 30 seconds.

Scare tactic spots highlight voter insecurities, either overtly or implied. Using fear as a vehicle has become a popular technique of persuasion in ads. (Beiler, c1986)

Analyzing the Political Advertisement

Students should look for and identify both techniques and ad type when analyzing political ads. Keep in mind that many ads combine numerous techniques and even ad types within a 30-second spot. Have the students watch for how the opponent is pictured/described or mentioned at all. Ensure they pay attention to props used, the backgrounds selected, what clothing is being worn (and by whom). They should also note the background audio/music and any text superimposed, crawled, or otherwise displayed. More difficult, but important, is for the students to evaluate the mood or tone of the ad—is it humorous, ominous, serious—and see if they can attribute a motive to that tone. For example, if the ad is ominous and foreboding, is it attempting to make viewers fear the opponent?

> **Political Ad Analysis Worksheet**
>
> Is a political ad negative? Warm and fuzzy? Visionary/biographical? Humorous? Scary? Does it advocate? Does it induce trust? I've created a worksheet that can aid students in analyzing political ads. Which type of ad? Audience targeted? Key images? Sounds used? Theme/slogan?
>
> This worksheet is downloadable: www.frankwbaker.com/adanalysisworksheet.htm.

There are a number of sources where you can find political ads for your students to analyze.

Resources for Political Ads

The Living Room Candidate

www.livingroomcandidate.org

> Presidential campaign commercials 1952–2008 from the Museum of the Moving Image

EASE History

www.easehistory.org/castream.asp?id=2

> Contains video clips from presidential campaigns 1952–2004

CNN Political Archives

www.cnn.com/ALLPOLITICS/1996/candidates/ad.archive/

> An archive of presidential TV ads

Power to Learn: Critical Viewing

www.powertolearn.com/themes_election2000new/criticalviewing_videos.html

> View Smart to Vote Smart, presented by The Family and Community Critical Viewing Project, offers insights and exercises to help teachers, students, and parents better understand the presentation of political messages.

Fact-Checking Political Messages

When politicians say something in their political advertising, how do you know if it's the truth? Many newspapers and TV news operations are now engaged in "Ad Watches." An *ad watch* involves a reporter's analysis and deconstruction of the words, images, and claims in a candidate's or organization's commercial. A typical ad watch will also include the actual script from the commercial.

During the 2010 national debate about health care reform, millions of dollars were spent on national and local spots designed to influence voters. An ad-watch column from *USA Today* that examined two such ads, "Ad watch: A closer look at dueling health care spots," can be accessed at www.usatoday.com/news/washington/2010-03-16-health-ads_N.htm.

Two new websites are also fact-checking claims. The first is FactCheck, (http://factcheck.org), operated by the nonpartisan Annenberg Public Policy Center. FactCheck analyzes not only what politicians say in speeches, but also what they say in their advertising. The second site is PolitiFact (http://politifact.com), managed by the *St. Petersburg Times* newspaper in Florida. One of the features of PolitiFact is the Truth-o-meter, which reveals whether a statement made is true, false, or somewhere in the middle. The site also features an Obameter that keeps up with promises the president made during his run for the White House, as well as a GOP Pledge-o-meter that does the same thing for Republicans in the House and Senate.

Advertising in the Health Classroom

Many researchers point to advertising as the culprit behind many of our health problems. Some consumer groups have even tried and have sometimes succeeded in restricting ads as one way to solve particular health issues. In 1971, all television advertising for tobacco ceased. However, advertising for tobacco products continues in other media, as does the marketing of junk food, body image, alcohol, sexual messages, and violent media.

Media-Related Health Standards

The National Health Education Standards (NHES) include Standard 2, which says:

> **Standard 2.** Students will analyze the influence of family, peers, culture, media, technology, and other factors on health behaviors. (www.cdc.gov/healthyyouth/sher/standards/2.htm)

The NHES document, released in 2007 by the Joint Committee on NHES with support from the American Cancer Society, makes references to both the "effect of media" as well as "how media influences" choices and decision-making.

Media-Smart Youth: Eat, Think, and Be Active! (www.nichd.nih.gov/msy) is an interactive, after-school education program for young people ages 11–13. It is designed to help teach youth about the complex media world around them and how it can affect their health—especially in the areas of nutrition and physical activity.

Weight-Loss Advertising

Research indicates that many young women do not apply critical thinking skills when it comes to advertising. Ads touting diet (weight-loss) solutions are a case in point. These ads show up most frequently around holiday times of year in hopes of preying on consumers who want to lose recently gained weight. In a 2002 analysis of weight-loss advertising (www.ftc.gov/bcp/reports/weightloss.pdf), the Federal Trade Commission warned about the deceptive nature of some advertising. Many ads feature the "before and after" photos of people who supposedly used the weight-loss product. The FTC analysis warns consumers that the "before" picture often portrays people with poor posture and neutral facial expressions, while the "after" picture often is brightly lit, featuring models who have good posture and a smiling face.

FIGURE 4.5 Typical before photos (sad, poor posture, and poorly lit) and after photos (smiling, good posture, and well lit).

The FTC has more advice for consumers: Don't believe everything you see, read, or hear. The commission calls many of these ads "deceptive" and is continually citing companies whose ads "cross the line." On its website (www.ftc.gov/bcp/edu/microsites/redflag), the FTC presents some of these weight-loss ads and helps consumers deconstruct the false claims and deceptive words and phrases.

Activities

Have students comb though their favorite magazines aimed at teens and young women. Have them remove any ads for weight-loss products and conduct an online search that might bring up news stories or other background information about the claims in the ads. Look for examples of deceptive claims made by the manufacturer.

Pick up almost any magazine featuring a model or actress on the cover, and you will find one common body size—the 100-pound woman. By some estimates, that "body image" represents less than 10% of American women, but it is the only one seen on most magazine covers. Students should be encouraged to deconstruct these images and, using many freely available Internet tools, create their own, more accurate, and realistic magazine covers.

An excellent tool for spurring discussion of media-driven body issues is the one-minute video, "Evolution," produced by the Dove soap company and available online (www.youtube.com/watch?v=hibyAJOSW8U). The spot uses time-lapsed photography to show a model, without makeup, sitting under the hot lights about to be made up.

Within seconds, with her hair styled, makeup applied, and her photo taken, her image has been imported into a computer, where a software editor begins to alter the image. We see her neck lengthened, eyebrows changed, and more. (For those who have only heard about digital-alteration software, now you get to see it in action.) The final image shows the altered model's face adorning a billboard as the camera pulls out to show us the neighborhood with people walking past it. The spot ends with the words on the screen: "No wonder our perception of beauty is distorted." This video alone should spark a discussion in classrooms about the ethics of digital manipulation.

Another good project, called "Your Own Healthy Style: A Middle-School Curriculum to Enhance Body Image," done as a project by the Montana Office of Public Instruction and Montana State University-Bozeman, can be found at http://opi.mt.gov/pdf/health/bodyimagecurr.pdf.

Sexual Media Messages

Like it or not, sex sells. Therefore, it can be found everywhere: from television and magazines to movies and websites. Many studies have examined the impact of these media messages on young people's attitudes and behaviors. One thing students can do is analyze the portrayal of sex in media to determine if outcomes are accurately portrayed.

I maintain a list of studies, readings, lesson plans, and other resources about this topic on my website, at www.frankwbaker.com/sex_in_media.htm.

Tobacco Advertising and Marketing

Today, the tobacco industry has to work harder than ever to get its message out. (Remember when the NASCAR races were sponsored by a tobacco brand and called the Winston Cup?) Since the 1998 Federal Tobacco Settlement, the marketing of tobacco products has been more restricted. For example, no longer will you find tobacco billboards or signs inside sporting events. But that doesn't mean that all advertising has been restricted. Take a look at the convenience store/gas station shown in Figure 4.6. The store is located on a highway that leads to a major university. Tobacco signs can be seen (left) facing the highway; (front) along a light pole, and (background) in the store windows. Can students tell how important it is for the tobacco industry to position its ads at this location?

FIGURE 4.6 Strategic placement of tobacco advertising.

Source: Photo by Frank W. Baker.

Activities

Assign students the task of documenting where they find tobacco ads in their neighborhoods. Or, using an online map, students could be assigned specific areas of a city. They should note the name of the store, its address, and what the surroundings are like. Students could create an interactive map of their city or town, indicating which brands are located in which parts of the municipality. By looking at "the big picture," can your students come to some conclusions about why certain brands are advertised in specific parts of a city? Ask them if there should be laws about how close tobacco ads can be to churches, playgrounds, or schools.

Recommended Curricula

Media Sharp
www.cdc.gov/tobacco/publications/dvds_videos/mediasharp

> This kit, put together by the Centers for Disease Control and Prevention, is an important new tool to help middle and high school youth evaluate media messages and make healthy, life-saving choices. It includes an entertaining, 7-minute video and an easy-to-follow teacher's guide loaded with activities, handouts, and discussion topics centered around the messages about tobacco and alcohol use that the media is sending.

The Media Straight Up!
http://medialiteracyguide.org

> This middle school curriculum was created by Drug Free Pennsylvania and Renee Hobbs of Temple University's Media Education Lab to help kids make more informed decisions, such as avoiding risky drug and alcohol-related behaviors while learning how traditional and online media influence society.

Deconstructing Ads and Counteradvertising

Figures 4.7a and 4.7b are designed to provide students with some guidance on what to look for when studying tobacco ads from magazines.

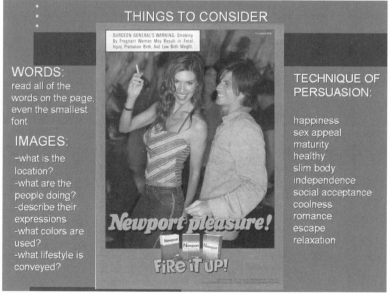

FIGURES 4.7a and 4.7b Deconstructing a cigarette ad.

Color version: www.frankwbaker.com/smokingprocedures.htm

Deconstructing a Cigarette Ad Activity

Have students go through magazines at home or at school to find examples of full-page ads for tobacco. Using the critical-thinking questions, have your students work in groups to analyze and deconstruct the ads' words, images, layout, subtext, and more.

Counteradvertising and Parody

After a discussion about the various tobacco ads, you can introduce your students to "counteradvertising," or parody. These messages go to extremes to poke fun at the original messages. It is easy to see how the original ad (Figure 4.8a) was altered to create the counter ad (Figure 4.8b).

Counter Ad Activity

Students can be encouraged to create their own "counter ads" by giving them paper, crayons/markers, scissors, and other manipulatives.

Working in groups, they should create one parody ad, after which they can share it with the rest of the class or post it on a class blog, wiki, or Ning site.

> **Counter Ad Examples**
>
> A number of other counter ad examples can be downloaded by going to my website: www.frankwbaker.com/counteradexamples.htm.

FIGURES 4.8a and 4.8b A cigarette ad and a parody of it.

Sample Deconstruction

The Media Literacy Project website (http://medialiteracyproject.org/deconstructions) features a "Deconstruction Gallery" that includes a number of ads that are already analyzed and deconstructed. With permission, we present their deconstruction of Camel's No. 9 "Stilletto."

Deconstructing Camel's No. 9 100's Ad

Who created this media message? Why? R.J. Reynolds Tobacco Company created this message to introduce its new product, Camel No. 9 Stiletto cigarettes. This version is a longer, thinner version of the regular No. 9s.

Who is the target audience? What text, images, or sounds suggest this? The target audience is probably women, ages 13–25. Marketing in general often encourages young women to be fashion conscious, and in this particular ad, the reference to a stiletto implies that these cigarettes are a fashion accessory, just like the high-heel shoe. The color pink, often associated with girls and femininity, is emphasized in the product packaging and is echoed in the pink stripes on the left side of the ad. The use of light pink flowers and lettering in the background also implies ideas of feminine identity. The packaging of the cigarette box and the name of the cigarette both mirror the packaging of Chanel No. 5 perfume for women. Chanel No. 5 is considered to be the most famous scent in the

Camel's No. 9 100's print ad, "Stiletto."

world, with the company claiming that a bottle is sold every 30 seconds. The ads have also been placed in glossy fashion magazines, such as *Vogue, Fashion Rocks,* and *Glamour,* which have high percentages of female readership.

What is the text (literal meaning) of the message? The text of the ad includes a white frame around a black background, two pink stripes on the left side, faded pink flowers and lettering in the background, and in the foreground an image of two black boxes of cigarettes—one with pink trim (regular) and the other with mint green trim (menthol). The words "Now available in Stiletto" are at the top of the page, and beneath the boxes of cigarettes, the ad reads, "No. 9 100's." The boxes of cigarettes have images of a pink camel on the front, and above it, the brand-name logo "Camel." The surgeon general's warning is in a white box in the bottom left-hand corner of the ad, ingredient information with a website is directly above it, and the copyright information is in the bottom right-hand corner.

What is the subtext (unstated or hidden message)? Camel No. 9 Stiletto cigarettes, and the women who smoke them, are feminine, sophisticated, glamorous, and sexy. Cigarettes are part of what it means to be a woman. Cigarettes are pretty. Cigarettes are a fashion accessory. Camel No. 9 really understands the needs of women smokers. Cigarettes are made from pink camels.

What kind of lifestyle is presented? Is it glamorized? How? A lifestyle of femininity and fashion is associated with stiletto high heels.

What values are expressed? The values expressed are sophistication, femininity, and fashion.

What tools of persuasion are being used?

> **Symbols.** The color pink and the flowers are used to symbolize femininity. The design of the box is used to symbolize a famous brand of perfume.
>
> **The Big Lie.** Cigarettes are not perfume and do not smell like perfume.
>
> **Simple Solutions.** The idea is that using this product will automatically make a young woman accessorized and sophisticated.
>
> **Diversion.** Pretty packaging is used to divert attention away from the fact that Camel No. 9 Stiletto cigarettes are just as deadly as any other brand.
>
> **Timing.** The Stiletto version was introduced to coincide with the fall fashion magazine spreads. (http://medialiteracyproject.org/deconstructions/camel-no-9-stiletto; http://medialiteracyproject.org/language-persuasion)

The Marketing and Advertising of Alcohol

Health education curricula also include an examination of the influence and effects of alcohol. Almost every state's standards include student study of the techniques used by alcohol advertisers. Sports programs, on both radio and television, are prime spots for advertising alcohol products. Alcohol advertising is also predominant in and around colleges and universities. An excellent curriculum for Grades 7–10 about alcohol advertising, which I recommend, is the Alcohol Policy Network's *Under the Influence?: Educator's Kit On Alcohol Advertising* (www.apolnet.ca/resources/pubs/arapo_kit.html).

The Economics of Advertising

Some time ago, I created a section on my website called "Math in the Media." I had read a news story that detailed the 10 most common ways that math could be found in the news. It listed such things as the movies (box office results), monthly government reports (the unemployment rate, Consumer Price Index), high school dropout rates, book sales (such as the *New York Times* best sellers), sports statistics, and stock market data

The website got me thinking about media, especially television, because I had previously worked in television news. Television is an advertiser-supported medium. Programs don't get on the air until they have first secured enough advertisers to fund the program's development. Once that program gets on the air, it must maintain a certain size of the audience, or it will go off the air.

Each week, Nielsen (the primary media-ratings company) releases a list of the highest-rated, nationally broadcast programs. Broadcast networks include ABC, CBS, FOX, and NBC. This list does not include cable programs because they are not broadcast. It also does not include local independent broadcasters because they aren't available nationally. You can see a sample Nielsen report in Figure 4.9.

Reading this chart is part of a media literacy exercise. We might first ask students: Who created this chart? Why was it created? and Who uses the information in this chart? Everything on the chart is pretty easy to understand without explanation, except for the column labeled Adults 18–49, which might be new and unknown to most readers.

Top primetime shows of the week
(March 8-14, 2010)

Rank	Skein (Net)	Adults 18-49 rating/share	Overall aud in millions
1.	**American Idol-Tue.** (Fox)	8.2/23	22.75
2.	**American Idol-Wed.** (Fox)	7.5/20	20.70
3.	**American Idol-Thu.** (Fox)	6.3/19	19.34
4.	**The Big Bang Theory** (CBS)	5.9/15	16.32
5.	**Two and a Half Men** (CBS)	5.8/15	17.61
6.	**House** (Fox)	4.8/13	12.81
7.	**Lost** (ABC)	4.2/11	9.49
8.	**Grey's Anatomy** (ABC)	3.9/11	10.94
8.	**How I Met Your Mother** (CBS)	3.9/11	10.06
8.	**Undercover Boss** (CBS)	3.9/10	13.51
11.	**NCIS** (CBS)	3.8/11	19.58

FIGURE 4.9 A sample Nielsen television report, pulled from *Variety* magazine, March 18, 2010, p. 15.

Adults 18–49 indicates the ages of the people watching television who are part of this ratings sample. Under the words "Adults 18–49" are the words "rating/share." First, we might ask students, what is a rating? A rating is a number (in this case, a percentage) that represents the number of people watching this particular program at this particular time. Here is the official definition of *rating* according to Nielsen (www.agbnielsen.net/glossary/glossary.asp):

> The average percentage of a given population group watching a TV channel/program across a set time interval. The concept of rating is generally restricted to TV, but may also be used for other media. One rating point equals 1 percentage.

So, for the number-one program that week (American Idol-Tue.), the national rating was 8.2. But what does that really mean? A little math is required. Nielsen says that one rating point equals roughly 1.32 million viewers of those ages 18–49. Students could use their math skills to determine the size of the audience. The last column indicates that the overall audience for "American Idol-Tue." was 22.75 million viewers. This number includes those under age 18 and those over age 49.

Next, we might ask students: What is a share? It is the percent of households using television (HUT) which are tuned to a specific program at a specified time. Shares are determined by taking the rating and dividing it by the total number of homes using TV. For "American Idol-Tue.," the share of audience is 23%. We can conclude that all the other shows airing at the same time as *American Idol* on Tuesday make up the remaining 77% of the audience.

Two important questions here are Who uses these numbers? and Why do they exist? Because television is a business, the people who buy time on programs (advertisers) need a way to measure the viewing audience. Ratings are the answer. Students could research the question: How are TV ratings measured? Who gets to see the numbers? What happens if the rating/share of a program starts to decline? What is the cost of a 30-second commercial within a program rated number 1 as compared to a program rated number 24? Have students contact a local TV station's sales department and determine the cost of a 30-second ad in a high-rated program.

Activity

Students might be asked to select a favorite genre (reality, sit-com, drama, etc.) and create a list of all programs within that genre. Compare and contrast the ratings and shares of all programs within that genre. Examine a list of all programs during a specific time period: compare and contrast the ratings and shares at that time. Make a list of all of the commercials aired during a specific program and a specific time: Can you come to any conclusions about who the audience might be, based on the commercials you've viewed?

Issues in Advertising

If you want to provide your students with some timely, relevant background readings on advertising in American society, I suggest the Media and Advertising section of the *New York Times*, the Advertising Industry News section of the *Wall Street Journal*, and *AdWeek*.

Advertising Resources

Current Issues in Advertising

New York Times Media & Advertising Section
www.nytimes.com/pages/business/media/

Wall Street Journal: Advertising Industry News
http://online.wsj.com/public/page/news-advertising-industry.html

AdWeek Magazine
www.adweek.com

Texts for Schools

A full list of recommended texts and videos for teachers and students
www.frankwbaker.com/advcon.htm

Websites

Admongo
www.admongo.gov

The Federal Trade Commission's advertising literacy site for tweens

AdViews
http://library.duke.edu/digitalcollections/adviews/

A digital archive of vintage television commercials

ADText
www.aef.com/on_campus/adtext/adtext_unit/landing

Advertising curriculum

Advertising's 15 Basic Appeals, by Jib Fowles
www.cyberpat.com/shirlsite/education/essay2/jfowles.html

Color and Meaning in Advertising
www.color-wheel-pro.com/color-meaning.html

Don't Buy It: Get Media Smart
http://pbskids.org/dontbuyit/about.html

A PBS ad-awareness site for kids

How to Teach Advertising
https://e-folio.web.virginia.edu/Q-folio/1/EDIS542/2006Fall-1/cs/UserItems/
hmj8y_1327.html

Looking at Advertising
www.kidcyber.com.au/topics/advertising.htm

A guide to analyzing television and print

Emergence of Advertising in America: 1850–1920
http://library.duke.edu/digitalcollections/eaa/

The Role of Advertising in America
www.ana.net/advocacy/getfile/15495

An overview by the Association of National Advertisers

Mediasmart: Teaching Materials on Digital Advertising
www.mediasmart.org.uk

Media Literacy Clearinghouse ad links
www.frankwbaker.com/ad_links.htm

Teaching Advertising with YouTube Videos
www.theadclass.com/education/using-youtube-to-teach-advertising-creativity

A collection of short clips from and about the advertising industry

CHAPTER 5

MOVING IMAGES

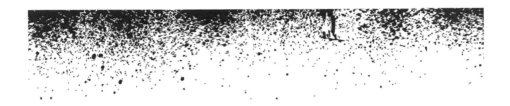

We live in a world of moving images. To participate fully in our society and its culture means to be as confident in the use and understanding of moving images as of the printed word. Both are essential aspects of literacy in the twenty-first century.

from the foreword of *Film: 21st Century Literacy*

Put cameras into the hands of young people and you have empowered them to tell stories and to create their own personal narratives. It's that simple. Using production-editing software (e.g., Final Cut Pro, iMovie; Windows Media Maker), students quickly learn how to edit and manipulate words, images, and sounds and begin to appreciate the process. Many educators and their students have already discovered the value of having students create "digital stories," "book trailers," and any number of worthwhile projects. In many ways, our students are more knowledgeable about how to create digital productions than their teachers. The so-called "digital natives" are already comfortable with the media and tools. The moving images of television and film provide a plethora of opportunities for us to meet standards, benchmarks, and objectives.

ELA Standards for Viewing

National Council of Teachers of English

NCTE Position Statement on Multimodal Literacies

There are increased cognitive demands on the audience to interpret the intertextuality of communication events that include combinations of print, speech, images, sounds, movement, music and animation. Products may blur traditional lines of genre, author/audience, and linear sequence. (www.ncte.org/positions/statements/multimodalliteracies, para. 22)

McREL Language Arts Viewing and Media Standards

Viewing Standard 9. Uses viewing skills and strategies to understand and interpret visual media

Level I (Grades K–2)

5. Knows different elements from films, videos, television and other visual media that appeal to him or her

6. Understands the similarities and differences between real life and life depicted in visual media.

ELA Standards for Viewing *(Continued)*

Level II (Grades 3–5)

3. Knows that film and television have features that identify different genres

Level III (Grades 6–8)

3. Knows typical genre of different visual media

5. Understands how language choice is used to enhance visual media

6. Understands how symbols, images, sound, and other conventions are used in visual media

8. Knows that people with special interests and expectations are the target audience for particular messages or products in visual media; and knows that design, language, and content reflect this

Media Standard 10. Understands the characteristics and components of media

Level II (Grades 3–5)

1. Knows the main formats and characteristics of familiar media

2. Understands similarities and differences among a variety of media

Level III (Grades 6–8)

5. Understands aspects of media production and distribution

Level IV (Grades 9–12)

6. Understands the influence of different factors … on media production, distribution and advertising

9. Understands the relationship between media and the production and marketing of related products.

Source: Selected standards reprinted by permission of McREL from *Content Knowledge: A Compendium of Standards and Benchmarks for K–12 Education.*

Continued

> ### ELA Standards for Viewing *(Continued)*
>
> ***National Film Study Standards:* The Story of Movies**
> (developed by The Film Foundation)
>
> > ***1.0 Film Language.*** Students learn to read and interpret visual text by developing a film vocabulary, identifying editing techniques, and analyzing film elements within selected scenes.
> >
> > ***2.0 Historical and Cultural Contexts.*** Students understand that a film is both a historical/social document and a cultural artifact. Students analyze social issues presented in film and form conclusions about the ways in which film influences and is influenced by the society in which it is produced.
> >
> > ***3.0 Production and Creative Expression.*** Students understand that film is an expression of a director's personal vision produced through a collaborative process. Students understand and distinguish the various filmmaking roles that contribute to the final work of art.
> >
> > ***4.0 Viewers' Response and Aesthetic Valuing.*** Students understand that a film is a work of art. Students describe, interpret, and analyze a film's visual design. They respond to and make informed judgments about film, deriving personal meaning from the work. They express their viewpoints through oral and/or written presentations.
> >
> > ***5.0 Cross-Curricular Connections.*** Students first tap their knowledge of other disciplines to study a film. They then apply what they have learned about film to other disciplines, making connections between film and literature/language arts, film and history/social studies, film and other arts, and film and sciences. (www.storyofmovies.org/pdfs/NationalFilmStudyStandards. pdf, p. 144)

Moving Images and Active/Critical Viewership

When we settle into our easy chairs to watch a television program at home or a film at the movie theatre, we just want to be entertained: we don't want to think. When teachers use video or film in the classroom, it is a signal to our students to "turn off" the thinking parts of their brains. But it doesn't have to be that way. Effective teachers know that they must prepare students before they use these kinds of media in instruction.

A spokesperson for the Jacob Burns Film Education Center in Pleasantville, New York, says the organization's mission is to foster these new thinking skills: "We believe that to be literate in the 21st century, one must know how to communicate not just with written and verbal 'texts,' but with visual and aural texts as well" (Daunic, 2010).

Television and Film

Before students can understand moving images, they must learn how to become active, critical viewers. In regard to film, it is known as "film literacy" or "film fluency." Critical viewing involves understanding what to look for and what to look at. It also means a clear understanding of the process of production. Part of the production process involves both writing scripts and creating storyboards. Another aspect of media production is understanding the "language of moving images." Asking questions of these kinds of media and understanding the language of the medium are the first steps to media literacy.

Moving Images as Texts

Another important thing to remember is that media (television, film) are texts designed to be read (analyzed) and produced. Even though most of our textbooks don't address media as texts, they are. Most teacher education programs don't include teaching about the media, but they should. Studying "media as text" involves analysis, deep reading, deconstruction, and production. Here I offer some ideas for incorporating moving-image texts, starting with commercials, then examining news, and lastly, analyzing film.

Getting Started with Moving Images: Toy Commercials

Perhaps no advertising is more persuasive, deceptive, or influential than the toy commercial. During the holiday time of year, these spots flood the airwaves, and young people pay attention: they beg parents and grandparents to "buy me that." Before starting to use and teach about toy commercials, it might be helpful to introduce the "language of moving images."

These are the tools and techniques used by producers of toy commercials to create their ads. Every year the Emmys and the Oscars honor people in television and motion pictures. If you're familiar with these awards ceremonies, then most likely you are familiar with the categories: Best Director, Best Cinematography, Art Direction, Original Screenplay, and so on. If you think for a moment about the people who make television, video, and film (or if you've ever watched the ending credits), then you know it takes hundreds of people to create a production.

Each one of these people specializes in some part of the production. Most likely, they've studied production and become experts in some aspect, like camerawork, lighting, or sound. These people know how to "tell a story" using tools and techniques, and they know how to communicate so that an audience will understand what is happening on the screen.

Think about the start of a movie, for example. It might begin with a wide-angle establishing shot of the skyline of New York City. The director is communicating that the action (story) takes place in the Big Apple. In the *Star Wars* films, the character Darth Vader is dressed in black—a signal that he is the bad guy. The choice to dress a character in a certain color has meaning to the viewing audience. The choice of camera shot and costume, in these examples, are just two of the tools and techniques that filmmakers use.

When we watch television and film, we don't always recognize that these techniques have meaning. So, as educators, we have opportunities to help students learn the language of moving images. Think for a moment about the story of "Jack and the Beanstalk." Imagine you are Jack looking up at the giant. You see the giant from your point of view (POV). Now imagine you're holding a camera, taking a picture of the giant. You have pointed your camera up. Photographers know that when you are positioned low, shooting up at someone, one of the things communicated is that the subject is not only larger but also more important. The reverse is also true: when you shoot down on someone, you make the person seem powerless and smaller. This rule is just one of many in photography and filmmaking.

Components of the Language of Moving Images

It would be helpful for students to keep the following "language of moving images" list in mind every time they are presented with video media messages:

Cameras. A camera can be positioned high or low; a camera can also be panned (moving left or right) or tilted (moving up or down); the lens can zoom in (closer) or pull out (farther away).

Lighting. This includes shadows, colors, and other lighting characteristics such as "soft" or "harsh" light, contrast, and more.

Audio. Sound includes who is heard speaking, what music is used, sound effects, volume, ambient sounds, and more.

Editing. Editing determines what is seen and not seen. Frequency and transition style between cuts are also part of editing.

Setting. The place where and time when the actions occur.

Actors. In addition to "who" they are, the language of actors includes their nonverbal expressions, makeup, hair style, accents, and style of speech.

Analyzing a Toy Commercial

As much as I am not a fan of these types of worksheets, I found that when I developed and used this one with young people, it helped them to focus on those elements in toy ads that they'd never noticed before. The worksheet and the lesson plan that follows it provide you an opportunity to "open the door" on these influential commercials. I think you will discover that your students will be anxious to share stories about some toy they received during the holidays or for their birthday that failed to live up to the promises made in the commercial (more about this later).

Introduce this worksheet by reviewing all of the items across the top row. Explain that you might have individual students or groups of students paying attention to one of the items. This allows them to focus on that item instead of the entire commercial.

As students watch commercials, they should fill in the blanks. For more information, go to www.frankwbaker.com/toys.htm.

TV Toy Ad Analysis Worksheet								
Name of toy/ manufac- turer	Techniques of persuasion	Target age/ gender	Age of kids in ad	Small print	Actor expressions	Memorable phrases or slogans	Visuals (lights, color, special effects)	Sound (including music)

Techniques of Persuasion			
Cool kids	Family fun	Excitement	Star power
Bigger is better	Repetition	Feel good	Sounds good
What's missing?	Weasel words	Cartoon characters	

WORKSHEET 5.1 TV Commercial Analysis Worksheet: TV Toy Ad.

Source: Baker, ©2005, www.frankwbaker.com/toys.htm

Because analyzing a television ad is a difficult concept with lots of choices, I've found it helpful to give a printout of the following list to the students responsible for tracking the common techniques of persuasion. I've adapted Lisa Thompson's list of advertising strategies (2003) from *Key Ingredients: America by Food*, published by the Smithsonian Institution as a Teacher's Guide.

Common Techniques of Persuasion/Advertising Strategies

Cool kids: Everybody wants to be these kids!

Family fun: This ad shows a product as something that instantly helps families have fun together.

Excitement: This product is the key to amazing fun and adventure.

Star power: A huge celebrity uses this product.

Bigger is better: This ad makes the product look bigger than it actually is.

Repetition: Manufacturers hope that if you see a product or hear its name a lot, you'll want it.

Feel good: This ad tells a story that makes you feel good.

Sounds good: Manufacturers use music and other sound effects to grab your attention and make the product appealing.

What's missing?: The ad doesn't give you the full story about the product.

Weasel words: Words like *helps* and *virtually* are vague and undependable. (See page 76 for more examples of "weasely" words.)

Cartoon characters: They help you remember a product by putting a face to it (example: Tony the Tiger)

Source: Thompson, 2003, p. 16; www.agclassroom.org/teacher/pdf/key_ingredients.pdf

Techniques and Tricks in Toy Commercials

In a toy commercial that I use, the student audience is introduced to a toy (Cinderella's Magical Talking Vanity). In preparing to watch the ad, I instruct my audience to be sure to notice how tall the toy is. During the playback we see two girls playing with the vanity. As you can see in Figure 5.1, a screen shot from the video ad, it is difficult, if not impossible, to judge how tall the child's vanity actually is because the girls are seen both seated beside and standing next to it.

FIGURE 5.1 How tall is the vanity?

After the commercial has ended, I fold out a visual representation of the toy that I have printed on poster paper (Figure 5.2). Students are surprised when they see how small the actual vanity is. Often, with the poster of the toy in the front of the room, I will invite a participant to come and kneel down in front of the poster, as if she were the actress in the commercial. I will ask the class to be the director: they have the camera. So now, a question might be, if we wanted the toy to look taller, how might we reposition our camera? We might place our camera low, shooting up.

> ### Deconstructing a Typhoon 2 Toy Commercial
>
> A downloadable lesson plan, complete with a video for you to use with students: www.frankwbaker.com/buy_me_that

FIGURE 5.2 Visual representation of the vanity next to the author.

Source: South Carolina Educational TV.

What's Real and What's Not?

A great question for students to consider while watching these slickly produced ads is: What is real and what is not real? In the case of the Cinderella Magical Talking Vanity spot, the little girls are dressed up, and when they begin to put on "make-up," certain colors are used. Specific music is playing in the background as sparkles start to appear around them. By calling attention to those techniques, we are raising awareness, encouraging critical thinking, and fostering healthy skepticism.

Media as Writing

Another way to teach how to "read" toy commercials is to introduce the concept that all media start out as writing. Students can be told: The company that makes the toy invites an advertising agency to provide ideas on how best to market or advertise the toy. In the case of the commercial, a copywriter had to write the words on a script before one inch of footage was ever shot.

In my work, I introduce the basic two-column script format:

Video	Audio
(everything that is seen)	(everything that is heard)

It is the script and its accompanying storyboard (visual representation of the action) that the director (and crew) will use to plan the actual production of the commercial. Here is what the Cinderella's Magical Talking Vanity script might look like:

Video	Audio
	(Woman's voice-over/Music in the background): A fairy tale awaits you with Cinderella's Interactive Talking Vanity.
	Insert the key to unlock the magic and Cinderella appears with a special message: "Would you like to go to a royal ball tonight with Cinderella?"
	Cinderella's Magical Talking Vanity lets you get ready like a real princess.
	Just follow the magical instructions: Don't forget to put on your perfume.
	With Cinderella's Magical Talking Vanity, you'll become the princess fairytales are made of.
	Batteries not included. Some assembly required. Armoire and dresser sold separately, by CDI.

Color version: www.frankwbaker.com/cinderella_toy_ad.htm

Toy Ads as Deception

Many older students will realize that advertising is designed to make products look better than they really are. In a workshop I conducted about toy ads, I used the word "deceptive." Wisely, a participant asked me what the word meant. This was a perfect learning opportunity; after defining it, I recommended that her teacher add the word to that week's vocabulary list.

Yes, toy ads are deceptive: they use tricks and techniques that many of us don't understand or recognize. Is that legal? Well, yes and no. Older students could be asked to research questions such as, Who in the federal government oversees children's advertising? (Answer: the Federal Trade Commission.) We might also ask students: Do the networks (Nickelodeon, Disney, Cartoon, etc.) and TV stations have any obligation to air commercials that tell the truth? Another question for students might be, Who could you write a letter to in order to complain about a misleading or deceptive toy ad? Might your students review toys, write and publish their reviews on a blog, wiki, Ning, or class website? Other than television and the Internet, how else are toy marketers using social networks and new Web 2.0 technologies to reach both parents and young people?

Public Service Announcements (PSAs)

Many of us have seen or heard public service announcements. They appear in newspapers, magazines, and on radio and television. Although we may not think of them as ads, they do advertise or promote an issue, idea, or organization. Those of you who have been around long enough may remember "Only You Can Prevent Forest Fires" (Smokey the Bear) or the "Fasten Your Seatbelt" campaign.

More recent campaigns have addressed drug abuse ("This Is Your Brain On Drugs," done by Partnership for a Drug-Free America) and crime ("Take a Bite out of Crime," featuring McGruff the Crime Dog). A great resource for print, radio, and video PSAs is the Ad Council site (www.adcouncil.org), where you can download and save many of the Ad Council public service announcements.

Activity

Download several print PSAs from the Ad Council website, or locate one of them from a popular magazine at home or at school. Using a blank, two-column script format, have your students work in groups to create a 30-second commercial script based on the print ad they've selected. Upon completion of their scripts, they should present (act out) the PSA to the entire class. Provided you have the equipment, students could also recreate the commercial.

The Ontario Ministry of Education provides a good lesson plan (Grades 4–6) centered around creating a storyboard for a PSA. You can see and download the lesson plan by going to www.media-literacy.ca/welcome/Ideas/Ideas.html, then scrolling down and clicking on "Media Lit. Document from the Ministry of Ed."

Deconstructing a TV Commercial

Here is a lesson plan I developed some time ago. For years, ever since I first saw this cell phone commercial, I have been using this ad in my media literacy workshops.

Most of our young people already own mobile (cell) phones—they're connected. But when we ask these same young people how the cell phone was first marketed, their answers provide a good background for what they are about to see.

We know that young people watch a lot of TV, and so we know they are exposed to a lot of commercials, even though they may skip through them. Teaching advertising is a great way to infuse media literacy, critical viewing, and higher-order thinking skills into instruction. We know our students are targets for all kinds of products and services. We know that advertisers use every trick in the book (techniques of persuasion) to make their products attractive, appealing, and believable. We also know that most students watch media passively. Media literacy, among other things, is designed to turn them into active, questioning thinkers/viewers.

Activity Introduction

For the most part, students have never been taught how to watch or deconstruct television. (For that matter, many educators have never had a minute of media literacy training.) This activity involves listening to and viewing a commercial for cell phones. Students will be encouraged to look deeply and to ask questions about the production techniques used to make the commercial. Most national and state standards for English/Language Arts include both "viewing" and "listening," so this activity can help educators fulfill those objectives.

Pre-Viewing Questions

Students should be challenged with questions, such as:

- Who creates commercials and for what purpose?

- What techniques do the creators use to make a product appealing?

- How do they know who might be their "target audience"?

- Which specific "techniques of persuasion" might be used in this ad?

- Which television shows will the creators buy time within to show the ad?

- How much does it cost to make an ad and to position it inside a prime-time program?

- How are camerawork, lighting, music, editing used to tell the story?

- How do I feel after seeing a commercial?

- How does it appeal to my emotions?

Viewing and Listening

First, ask your students to close their eyes while you play back the one-minute ad found at www.youtube.com/watch?v=rb9XVKSb1XU.

Step 1. At the end of the minute, ask them to open their eyes and write down everything they heard. Why is this important? Most of us are visual learners, yet commercials are composed of both visuals and sounds. This exercise is designed to get them to think about the audio (sound) portion of what they experience. Give your students about a minute to make their list. After the minute, you should ask:

What did you hear? Be prepared to write their responses on the board, overhead, or whiteboard.

Invariably, some students may have heard things in the commercial that others in the class did not hear. For example, ask how many heard the wolf (or dog) howling? For those who did not hear it, you can point this out in step 2.

Step 2. Be prepared to play the commercial a second time, this time allowing them to see it for the first time. Before doing so, ask your students this question: Other than cell phones, what else is being sold? (This question is designed to get them thinking about how the creator of the cell phone ad used techniques to sell them.) After the second viewing, ask students the question: What else is being sold? (Did they answer "fear"?) Why would cell phone makers use fear to sell their products? What techniques did they use to "sell" fear? (Students should think about specific words, phrases, sounds, music, etc.) Can they think of any people who have used fear to sell products, concepts, issues, or candidates?

Introduce students to the languages of television/video production—these are the tools producers use not only to create media, but also to create meaning. Introduce these before proceeding.

Languages of Television/Video Production

Cameras. Where is the camera positioned (close-up, far away)? Does the lens zoom in or out? Does the camera tilt, pan, track?

Lighting. What time of day is depicted? What clues tell you so?

Music. What types of instruments do you hear?

Sounds. Other than music, what other sounds are heard?

Setting. Where is the location? Is it artificial or real? Justify your response.

Post-production. What impact does the editing have?

Actor's expression. Other than words, notice how an actor communicates via facial expressions, body language, and gestures.

Step 3. If you have time, play the commercial a third time and assign groups of students to one of the languages of television/video production. They will be responsible for discussing the ad from their group's assignment.

Because students will only be responsible for a single aspect of production, you should expect much more detailed answers.

First set of group discussion questions:

- How many close ups? Medium shots? Wide shots?

- Why is lighting important? How does it help to set the mood?

- Describe the music—does it remind you of something?

- How do sound effects contribute to the feel of this spot?

- What is the setting? How do you know? Is it realistic?

- How many edits? (Count the number of times the shot changes. Students should count out loud.)

For instance, the groups should discuss how many close-ups, medium-, and wide-angle shots there were or how the lighting shifts and why. When discussing the music, students can discuss the tempo, the instruments, what the music reminds them of. The sound-effects group can talk about the various sounds, the prominence of the ambient sound, and how it sets the mood. The setting group should discuss how "realistic" or abstract the setting is, how clues are placed to imply a setting, and so on. The editing group should count the number of edits and discuss how editing pace affects the message and mood. The actors group should discuss both the seen and unseen (narrator) actors and discuss what emotions they seem to be conveying beyond the words.

After this screening and after students have discussed their aspects of production, you might ask them about what happens at the end of the commercial. Why do they think the producer of the commercial stopped it like that? Ask them what they think might happen next. Have them discuss who has power, who lacks power, and how that dynamic works in the commercial.

Second set of group discussion questions:

- What is the impact of quick edits?

- What nonverbal expressions are used that might reveal how the actress is feeling, what she is thinking?

- What happens at the end of the commercial? Why do you think the producer of the commercial stopped it like that? What do you think might happen next?

- Power: Who has power, and who is powerless in the ad? How does that make you feel?

Optional step. Have your students recreate the actual script for this commercial. Download a blank script template from www.frankwbaker.com/blank_script_form. htm. In the "video" column they should make a list of each shot and describe it in detail. In the "audio" column, they should document everything that is heard.

News Literacy

When you or your students sit down to watch the news, you're probably not thinking about how the news reporter packaged or "edited" the story. But media literacy involves understanding how this was put together. "News literacy" is about helping today's young people better understand the processes that both print and broadcast journalists go through when they gather, produce, and report the news.

If we can understand how journalists go about their jobs, we might better appreciate the lengths to which they go to bring the news to us, whether that news is local or a thousand miles away. Howard Schneider, the dean of the School of Journalism at Stony Brook University, defines news literacy as "the ability to use critical thinking skills to judge the reliability and credibility of news reports, whether they come via print, television, or the Internet" (Schneider, 2009). One thing that Schneider wants his students and all news consumers to consider is "what neighborhood are you in?" He means to get us to think about the source of the information we are receiving. For example, he asks, are you in the news neighborhood, the editorial (opinion) neighborhood, the advertising (propaganda or publicity) neighborhood, or the gossip or features neighborhood?

Schneider's advice is good: it helps us distinguish between what is news and what is not. You can learn more about news literacy and hear Dean Schneider here: www.youtube.com/watch?v=RRysR0TMQj4.

News comes in many forms: the newspaper, news magazines, hourly news radio broadcasts, network TV news, cable TV news channels, and online news. No matter where you get your news, critical thinking about what you consume is essential. A new college-level course at Stony Brook University in New York is helping students analyze the news-gathering and news-delivery process. During my visit there, I saw students involved in the deconstruction of a broadcast news story. The professor introduced the story, from ABC's *World News Tonight* broadcast, and asked students to consider what was omitted from the story.

News Activities

You might want to try this activity with your students. From the ABC News archives, I downloaded the 2006 video story entitled "End of an Era" about the last Ford Taurus rolling off the Atlanta assembly line. Before introducing the actual news report, I ask students to assume the role of reporters. It is the reporter's job to tell the story, to decide who to interview, and to decide what images will help support the telling of the story. I ask students to assume that the news director sent them down to the Ford auto assembly plant where it's their job to conduct interviews with people about the final Ford Taurus. Who would they interview? What questions would they ask? Have students brainstorm and create a list of the people they might talk to on-camera.

Once your students have exhausted their list, show them the story found here: www.youtube.com/watch?v=CwuCm8hNXgI. After watching the Charles Gibson lead-in and the story, ask students: Who did ABC News *not* interview? Did ABC News do a good job with this story, or did they leave out an important interviewee? Have the students brainstorm reasons why some interviews may not have been done.

Take a news story from the morning's newspaper or from an online news source and have students recreate the story as a 30-second radio news script and as a one-minute television news script. You can even create a page with 140 blank spaces on it and ask them to create a "tweet" based on the story. How does each differ? What salient information will they include and exclude? Once students take part in such an activity, they begin to see the limitations (such as time) that broadcast news operations operate within.

The Importance of Sound in News Stories

Today, more and more forms of print journalism (magazines, newspapers) are turning to video to connect with audiences. Reporters and freelance writers are carrying video cameras and sound equipment. In addition to writing the story for print, they are also using the tools of video editing to tell a story that might appeal to a different audience. What follows is an example of the importance of sound in an edited news piece. A reporter and photographer for Minneapolis's *Star Tribune* newspaper shot the story of a mother about to be deployed for a tour of duty in Iraq. In addition to interviewing her, they also interviewed her young son.

The photographer wrote about her choice of music in the editing of their story on Poynter.org (a website for professional journalists). Go here: www.poynter.org/content/content_view.asp?id=160295 to view the video story with no music and then watch two more versions, each with a different musical selection. Ask your students how they feel after watching the different versions. Does the change in musical selections change the way they feel?

Go behind the scenes to see what happens in a television news room. Go to http://tiff.net/learning/resourcing/medialiteracycurriculum and launch "Behind the Scenes of a News Room" video. Download the accompanying study guide, "Developing a News Broadcast Study Guide," from the same site.

The Journalism Education Association's website (wee.jea.org/curriculum/) also includes links to several curricula related to journalism.

Follow issues in news and journalism with these timely resources: *Broadcasting & Cable Magazine* (www.broadcastingcable.com), Poynter Online (www.poynter.org), Pew Research Center's Project for Excellence in Journalism (www.journalism.org), and Project Censored (www.projectcensored.org).

Before Teaching the Language of Film

As stated previously, many of us watch film passively, with the thinking part of our brains turned off. Yet media literacy, including film literacy, involves turning on our thinking brains. Here is an idea about how to get your students thinking while watching film. This activity involves a close viewing of the opening six minutes of Steven Spielberg's *E.T.: The Extra-Terrestrial*. Most of us have seen it: E.T. is out in the woods collecting plants for the botanical garden that is inside the alien space-ship. But the arrival of some mysterious humans puts E.T. on the run, and he misses his appointment to meet up with the "mother ship," thus stranding him on Earth. You can find the entire scene online at www.youtube.com/watch?v=01ZMLzNbp-I.

For this assignment, play the clip, stopping it when E.T. watches the mother ship take off. Next, inform students that they will be given an assignment to view and listen to the clip again, but this time, they will have some specific things to pay attention to. Photocopy, cut out, and distribute the 12 Film Analysis Cards (Figure 5.3 or downloadable from www.frankwbaker.com/Film Analysis Cards.doc), giving one card to each group. Have them pass it around so that everyone in their group understands what they're to be paying attention to.

Play the film clip again. Students should take notes during this second playback. At the conclusion of the clip, give them time to consult and discuss what they saw and heard. After a few minutes, a representative from each group should discuss the group's findings with the entire class. Now that you've provided them with some aspect of the film to pay close attention to, they will be more literate the next time they watch a film. They'll be aware of the techniques filmmakers use (the language of moving images) and better understand what they see and hear on the screen.

Film Analysis Cards 1–6

LIGHTING

What time of day is it?

What are the clues?

What effect does lighting have?

Use two or three adjectives
to describe the lighting.

SOUND EFFECTS

Close your eyes.

You are only to listen to the scene,
after which you will be asked
to make a list of everything you
heard, and then share.

MUSIC

Describe the music at the
beginning, middle, and end
of the scene.

What happens and why?

How does the music contribute
to the mood or feel?

Is the music effective?

CAMERA: MOVEMENT

Document when the
director/cinematographer uses
a pan (left or right move), a tilt
(up or down move), or a
crane shot (high above).

What is the purpose of
these actions?

EDITING

Most of us never notice editing,
but it is important.

Count the number of edits
in this scene.

What impact does editing have?

CAMERA: LENS

Document when the
director/cinematographer
uses zooms (in or out).

Why are these shots used
when they are?

Film Analysis Cards 7–12

MOOD

What mood does this scene
put you in?

How do you feel?

Why do you feel this way?

What has the director done
to push your emotional buttons?
(be specific)

NONVERBAL LANGUAGE:
ACTOR EXPRESSIONS

Notice the expressions on the faces
of each of the actors.

Watch for any changes.

Be prepared to discuss
their expressions and what
they might mean.

SCENERY

Make specific notes about
what you see.

For example, where is the setting?

What are the clues?

What does the director allow
you to see?

Is the scene believable or not?

CLOTHES

What are the characters wearing?

How do their clothes communicate
what might be happening to them?

How might their clothes be related
to the plot or action?

COLOR

What colors do you see?

Where is color used or not used?

Why do you think a specific
color was used?

How does it make you feel?

CAMERA: POSITION

Document when the
director/cinematographer
uses a wide shot, a medium shot,
and a close-up.

FIGURE 5.3 Analysis Cards: Film. *Photocopy, cut out, and distribute cards to groups.*

Source: Baker, ©2005, www.frankwbaker.com/Film Analysis Cards.doc

Understanding the Filmmaking Process

Filmmakers don't just go out and shoot their film: they follow a process—a series of steps. You might even call it a formula. But because most of us have never had any "film education," we are not aware of the production process. Part of the filmmaking process involves writing a script, which is known as a "screenplay" in motion-picture language. But the script format for film does not resemble the two-column script for television introduced earlier. There are two major components of every screenplay: action and dialogue.

Figure 5.4 is a page from a real screenplay: We might ask students to notice the format of a screenplay and how to read it.

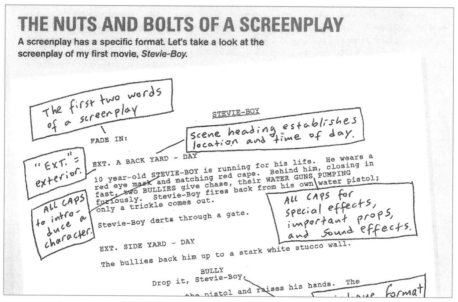

FIGURE 5.4 An annotated page from a screenplay by Steven Frank.

Source: Frank, 2007, *Writing! Weekly Reader 14+,* February/March, p. 15.

Students should identify both the *action* (what takes place in the story, how it unfolds) and the *dialogue* (the spoken words of the characters in the story). Parts of the screenplay are annotated (by the information in the boxes). Why do you think some words are in all capital letters? Which words are capitalized?

Storyboards

Storyboards are "visual representations" of the action that occurs in the screenplay. The film's art director or storyboard artist will use the script to create a picture of what that action might look like. The boards, as they are called, are then used by the director and the cinematographer (and others) to plan the actual shooting of the film. Storyboards are important because they help filmmakers see what the film might look like before even an inch of footage is shot. Figure 5.5 shows a template for a blank storyboard. The boxes are for the artist's rendition of the shots that comprise a scene, while the spaces below the boxes are for any technical directions or instructions the artist wishes to provide to the director (an others) about the placement of actors, lights, audio, and so forth.

Screenplays as Schoolwork

"If video is how we are communicating and persuading in this new century, why aren't more students writing screenplays as part of their schoolwork?"

—Heidi Hayes Jacobs, education consultant and author

FIGURE 5.5 A blank storyboard template.

Source: http://garrettmedia.com/mission/mission_images/thumbnails_storyboard_blank.jpg

Activity

Here is an exercise to get students to think visually about what they read and to create storyboards based on the first two pages of a novel. The two pages of Kate DiCamillo's novel *Because of Winn-Dixie* (2001) can be read on amazon.com. Divide the class into three groups. After reading the first two pages of Chapter 1, ask students what was happening in their brains while they were reading. Most will say they were visualizing the action from what they read. At this point, I would tell them that they are all filmmakers, because those who make film also visualize the action based on a story or a script. Next, I would ask students if they know how films are made. Some will know; others won't.

Films are scripted and then storyboarded before production starts. You can introduce them to the film-screenplay format and also to storyboarding. With the class divided into three groups, have each group create a storyboard of the grocery store scene, except ask each group to draw their boards from a different character's point of view (POV).

Group 1 will storyboard the scene from the POV of the store manager. Group 2 will storyboard the scene from the POV of Opal. Group 3 will storyboard the scene from the POV of the dog. Distribute a blank storyboard form to each group. They will need about 15 minutes to create their boards. Upon completion, a representative from each group will share the group's boards with the entire class. Finally, if you have a copy of the film based on the novel, you might cue it up and show how the filmmakers shot this scene. Some time ago, I communicated with Steve Werblun, the storyboard artist for the film, and he agreed to share some of his boards (see Figure 5.6).

Many DVD versions of films now include extra features, such as "the making of," "behind the scenes," "movie trailer," "storyboards," "director commentary," "sample pages from the screenplay," and more. These extras can be useful in helping students appreciate the language of film. I've created a list of DVDs you might wish to acquire at www.frankwbaker.com/dvd_project.htm.

FIGURE 5.6 Copies of actual storyboards from the movie *Because of Winn-Dixie*.

Source: Steve Werblun, storyboard artist.

Moviemaker Techniques to Make Us Believe Things

When we watch movies we sometimes ask ourselves, Is this believable? Could this have happened? And many times, the answer is yes. Filmmakers work hard to make everything in the movie believable, from the actors playing the characters to the film sets designed to look like the time portrayed in the film. Films comprise many elements. Here are some examples of films to illustrate major elements.

Use of Flashback in the Movie Titanic

Many young people believe this 1997 movie to be a true story. They don't recognize one of the film techniques used (flashback), which makes it appear to be a factual account. But this *Titanic* movie is not true; it is a work of fiction. Film director James Cameron created a lot of buzz with this movie. Most people already know the story of the "unsinkable" cruise ship that struck an iceberg on its maiden voyage in 1912, sinking in the frozen Atlantic Ocean waters, killing more than 1,500 people. Another 500 survived.

The sunken remains of the *Titanic* have been documented many times by deep-sea scientists and researchers. The photos and videos they've brought back create a haunting reminder of this disaster. In *Titanic*, the screenwriter wraps the true story of the ill-fated voyage around the fictional love story between a stowaway, Jack (played by actor Leonardo DiCaprio), and Rose (portrayed by actress Kate Winslet), a wealthy woman about to be married. Part of the story is told in flashback, a cinematic device in which someone recalls an earlier time. In this case, we meet Rose as an older woman, one of the last survivors. She reminisces about the ship and her relationship with Jack on the disastrous voyage.

When you look at Figure 5.7, you'll see how the *Titanic* director used the technique of a "dissolve" to communicate a passage of time or change in location. Director Cameron shows Jack and Rose embracing on the bow of the *Titanic*. Then one picture fades slowly away while another picture appears, thanks to the "dissolve" effect. The audience sees the "real" *Titanic* with Jack and Rose slowly fade away, while a new picture appears, showing actual footage shot with an underwater camera. By dissolving from the real ship to this one, Cameron takes the audience into the story and makes us believe that what we are seeing is real.

FIGURE 5.7 Titanic director James Cameron uses the dissolve effect to deepen his story and make it seem more real.

Source: www.angelfire.com/ga/wkb/titanic.html

Analyzing Authenticity in King

The miniseries *King* was broadcast by NBC over three nights in 1978. Shown in color, the series starred actor Paul Winfield as Martin Luther King, Jr. Analyzing the opening scenes of *King* will help students understand the various techniques director Abby Mann used to make the motion picture look authentic.

The frame grab from the opening scenes (see Figure 5.8) shows Dr. King (portrayed by Winfield) and a number of close associates being hustled by a loud, screaming mob in a city scene. The choices made by the director affect how we see and understand what is happening. The opening scene is shot in black and white. The actors resemble the real people they portray. The camerawork is handheld, allowing us, the audience, to be very close to the action. The film is grainy. As Dr. King is being hustled away from the obviously hostile crowd, we hear glass breaking. Dr. King is quickly put into a car parked nearby and, as the car drives away, the camera zooms in for a close-up on his face as he looks out the window to see people being hassled by law enforcement authorities. The cutaways to people on the street resemble newsreel footage of the time, although it is a reenactment, made to look like real television news coverage of the time.

This was the objective of the director and the cinematographer. Later in the film, actual newsreel footage is used, but unsuspecting viewers would not know which is real and which is not. When this film was released, the genre was described as a *docudrama*—the blending of the genres of documentary and drama.

FIGURE 5.8 From the opening scenes of *King*.

Source: NBC.

Docudramas

Benicia d'Sa discusses analyzing docudramas to teach history in *Social Studies in the Dark: Using Docudramas to Teach History* (2005):

http://worldroom.tamu.edu/Presentations/Making History Come Alive/ Making History Come Alive CD/Articles/Media Literacy/ Social Studies in the Dark, Using Docudramas.pdf

Understanding Symbolism: To Kill a Mockingbird

The opening credits in the film *To Kill a Mockingbird* allow students a good opportunity to study symbolism. Some students don't understand what symbolism is or how it is used, so teachers may have to spend more time on helping students appreciate it. Most students know that in both the novel and the film, the action takes place in Alabama during the Depression and that the story is told through the eyes of a child named Scout. The opening film credits are superimposed over a shot of a cigar box, and we see a child's hand open the box and begin to play with the objects inside (Figure 5.9).

Play the opening scene, which can be found at www.youtube.com/ watch?v=rP5MutuPVxk. (Note: The music used on this YouTube video is not the same as the original music composed for the film, so you may wish to play this clip without sound or to play the original opening scene.)

Unsuspecting viewers may not know that each object has some significance. It is up to us to recognize and identify each object and to understand what it symbolizes. As Professor of English and film William Costanzo has written:

> The objects that appear behind the opening credits include a pocket watch, harmonica, pearl necklace, whistle, marbles, and a child's drawing of a bird—items that gain meaning as the story unfolds. The sequence is a good introduction for the story's symbolism and themes. It also shows (to quote author Harper Lee) how a film can have "a life of its own as a work of art." Notice how the camera moves in, like a child's vision, to close-ups of these valued objects, tracking from left to right along the row of treasures carefully arranged. Notice how the nostalgic music and humming of a child create a mood. And notice what happens to the drawing at the end of the sequence. (Costanzo, 1997)

Activity

Students should pay careful attention to the opening sequence in the film. Some of the objects shown in that sequence are pictured in Figure 5.9. For each object/symbol, students should determine what is happening in the scene with the object and what it might mean or represent.

To learn more about the language of film and *To Kill a Mockingbird*, download the entire film study guide posted at www.frankwbaker.com/tkam.htm.

FIGURE 5.9 Opening credits from *To Kill a Mockingbird*.

Point of View in To Kill A Mockingbird

One way to help students understand point of view is to ask them to pay attention to where the camera is positioned. The courthouse scenes in *To Kill a Mockingbird* (see Figure 5.10) provide a good opportunity to have students answer the questions: Where is the camera? From whose point of view is this seen?

A general POV.

The jury's POV.

The POV of those seated in the balcony.

The judge's POV.

FIGURE 5.10 Courthouse scenes from *To Kill a Mockingbird.*

Motion Picture Analysis Worksheet

The one-page motion picture analysis worksheet developed by the education staff of the National Archives in Washington, D.C., might also be helpful to you and your students as they begin to analyze how films are made. You can find it at www.archives.gov/education/lessons/worksheets/movie.html.

Using Glogster to Create an Online, Interactive Poster

Glogster (www.glogster.com) is a useful creation tool that educators and their students have discovered. Using *To Kill a Mockingbird* as the example, I created a "glog" (see Figure 5.11) which includes a title, images from the film, a link to a YouTube video, a "speech bubble," a screen grab, a film poster, and the URL for my film-study guide. See the actual glog poster at http://medialiteracyman.glogster.com. Having students use glogster to create their own posters is another way of engaging them in producing a media text.

FIGURE 5.11 My *To Kill a Mockingbird* glog.

Film Industry Resources

Students can follow issues and developments in the film business through these resources:

Variety
 www.variety.com

Hollywood Reporter
 www.hollywoodreporter.com

Entertainment Weekly
   www.ew.com/ew/movies

Reel Movie News
   www.reelmovienews.com

Teaching Documentaries

Each year, The Discovery Channel broadcasts *Shark Week*, a series of programs that brings huge audiences to the network. While many of us enjoy these programs, we may not be aware that they are documentaries: the producers of each program have a point of view and a purpose. Many teachers have found success using documentaries to teach such concepts as point of view, audience, film technique, and more. Documentary filmmaker Liz Miller (in Winton, 2010) urges educators to think about the advantages of teaching with and about documentaries:

> Documentary has a critical role to play in education. The rapid advances in media technology have forced educators like myself to rethink notions of literacy and adapt our curricula accordingly. If students are watching, listening, and producing even more than they are reading, we must ensure they have critical frameworks for analysis. We can use documentaries to raise questions around voice, truth, ethics, and a range of themes relevant to the shifting literacies of the 21st Century. (http://artthreat.net/2010/03/documentaries-teaching-tool, para.11)

Many cable television networks broadcast "docs," as they're known. Pull up the schedules for PBS, HBO, the Discovery Channel, and other channels, and you will find a host of titles that could be used in instruction about documentaries. Networks such as the Independent Film Channel, Current TV, and the Documentary Channel also regularly feature docs. Like other films, docs don't have to be used in their entirety: many teachers report success identifying and using short clips to help students understand a particular theme or concept.

Many documentary films—some of them controversial—have also been the subjects of news stories, so many students may have heard of them, even if they haven't seen them. Some that come to mind include *Triumph of the Will* (Leni Riefenstahl); *Harvest of Shame* (Edward R. Murrow); *An Inconvenient Truth* (Davis Guggenheim); *Super Size Me* (Morgan Spurlock); *Fahrenheit 9/11* and *Bowling for Columbine* (Michael Moore); *The Civil War*, *Baseball*, *Jazz*, and *The War* (Ken Burns).

Critically Viewing Documentaries

As your students prepare to watch docs, they should be encouraged to answer a number of questions: What are documentaries? Who creates them, and for what purposes? What are the steps/stages to getting docs written and produced? How are they distributed? Where might you find them? How do docs differ from other films? What techniques are used in documentaries that may not be used elsewhere? Can documentaries be considered propaganda? Who are the audiences for docs?

For more on teaching documentaries, I suggest the book *Reading in the Reel World: Teaching Documentaries and Other Nonfiction Texts* by John Golden (2006). To locate other books and resources, and to download some recent articles, go to the section of my website called Using Documentaries in the Classroom: www.frankwbaker.com/using_docs_in_the_classroom.

Moving Images Resources

Books

A complete list of book recommendations for students and teachers
> www.frankwbaker.com/film_texts_k12.htm

Online Magazines and Journals

Screen Education
> www.metromagazine.com.au/screen_ed/

Film Score Monthly
> www.filmscoremonthly.com/

Script Magazine
www.scriptmag.com

Creative Screenwriting Magazine
www.creativescreenwriting.com

Cinefex, a visual effects magazine
www.cinefex.com

Digital Content Producer.Com
http://digitalcontentproducer.com

Videomaker
www.videomaker.com

Videography
www.videography.com

Other Online Resources

Interpreting Intertextuality: Analyzing Video Messages, by Luke Rodesiler.
Classroom Notes Plus. April 2010, NCTE (Available from www.ncte.org/journals/cnp/issues/v27-4)

Movie-Making in the Classroom, by Beth Newingham
http://blogs.scholastic.com/top_teaching/2010/01/movie-making.html

Commercials as Content–7 Places to Watch Ads on Purpose, by Josh Catone
www.readwriteweb.com/archives/commercials_as_content_-_7_pla.php

The State of the News Media: An Annual Report on American Journalism
www.stateofthemedia.org/2010/

Watching TV News: How to Be a Smarter Viewer. An online course taught by Marcy McGinnis and Howard Schneider
www.newsu.org/courses/watching-tv-news-how-be-smarter-viewer-0

Know the News Challenge Learning Guide, by Paul Mihailidis. KnowTheNews.tv
www.linktv.org/knowthenews/resources/learning/challenge

Media Literacy: Reading Between the Frames
www.oscars.org/education-outreach/teachersguide/medialiteracy/

Digital Storytelling Resources
www.tech-head.com/dstory.htm

Film: 21st Century Literacy
www.21stcenturyliteracy.org.uk/FilmLiteracyHiRes.pdf

IFC Film School Curriculum
http://screensite.org/ifc-film-school-curriculum

Media literacy tips and guides from Toronto International Film Festival (TIFF)
http://tiff.net/learning/resourcing/medialiteracytips

Using Documentaries in the Classroom
www.frankwbaker.com/using_docs_in_the_classroom.htm

Visual Storytelling through Lighting, by Sudeep Rangaswamy of Pixar Animation Studios
www.frankwbaker.com/visual_storytelling_through_lighting.htm

Recording and Saving Video Clips

Teaching media literacy has always been about analyzing and deconstructing media texts, including those on television and film. As Melinda Barlow puts it, a video clip "provides a concrete focal point for discussion and encourages interaction, especially when framed with a thought-provoking question or a pertinent quotation drawn from an assigned reading" (2011). Access to nonprint texts has not always been easy for teachers. With the advent of YouTube, TeacherTube, and the like, more educators have access, but many schools block that access, and many K–12 educators are not aware of how easy it is to record and retain these clips for later playback.

Today, appropriate use of video or film in the classroom means using "clips" or selected snippets of television programs, commercials, documentaries, or films. But the problem has always been: How do you capture and save just that brief scene? As a long-time media literacy educator (who began his career in the world of 3/4-inch video tape), I have sought solutions to problems of accessing and playback for many years. In the past, this meant traveling with a dozen (or more) such videos. I would carefully pack VHS tapes in my suitcase, hoping (and praying) they survived the trip. Often times, they did not.

The advent of the DVD was another milestone: Educators could, with random access, at least, skip to the designated chapter and fast-forward a DVD to get to the appropriate scene. But, as many of you know, this can be time-consuming.

Several years ago, I located a piece of hardware that solved this problem. The product, WinTV, is manufactured by Hauppauge (www.hauppauge.com). In essence, this device is a TV tuner that takes its signal from my cable-connected VCR/DVD combo player, and sends that signal to my computer. I can "watch" TV on a window on the desktop, and I can also record from television, VHS, or DVD. My model is the WinTV USB2 model. I paid around $100 at a Best Buy store. Newer versions are smaller and allow you to watch HDTV. Setup and connections are user-friendly.

Although I've been very satisfied with my Hauppauge, there are many quite similar devices that can perform the same tasks. *PCWorld* magazine has an informative article and multiple reviews of these devices at www.pcworld.com/article/118799/tv_tuners_for_your_pc.html. CNET (http://reviews.cnet.com/tv-adapters/) also has a huge archive of television-tuner device reviews for Windows and Macintosh systems.

A Note about Copyright

By now, you're probably asking: Is this legal? Because I am using these clips for analysis, interpretation, and deconstruction, it is legal. I base this on my reading and understanding of the transformative use of media under the "Fair Use" guidelines. For more information, I recommended reading *The Cost of Copyright Confusion for Media Literacy* (www.centerforsocialmedia.org/sites/default/files/Final_CSM_copyright_report_0.pdf) and *The Code of Best Practices in Fair Use For Media Literacy Education* (www.centerforsocialmedia.org/fair-use/related-materials/codes/code-best-practices-fair-use-media-literacy-education). You may also want to check with your school media specialist to see if your school or district has guidelines for media use.

CHAPTER 6

REPRESENTATION, BIAS, AND STEREOTYPES

Our children must learn how to spot a stereotype, isolate a social cliché, and distinguish facts from propaganda, analysis from banter, and important news from coverage.

—Ernest Boyer, former president of the Carnegie Foundation for the Advancement of Teaching

The classroom is a perfect place to help students begin to understand how the media work. Media are powerful: They set the agenda, and they tell us how to think and what to believe. But media literacy is designed to teach "healthy skepticism," to help our students not believe everything the media tells them. Here are a few more ideas about teaching students how the media work.

Representation

Representation is a concept that many students in American schools don't know because, again, they haven't been taught. What is representation?

> The media don't just offer us a window on the world. They don't just present reality, they represent it. Media producers inevitably make choices: they select and combine, they make events into stories, they create characters, they invite us to see the world in a particular way. Media offer us versions of reality. But audiences also compare media with their own experiences, and make judgments about how far they can be trusted. Media representations can be real in some ways and not in others: we may know that something is fantasy, yet it can still tell us about reality. (Buckingham, 2003, p. 8)

In the last line above, David Buckingham could very well have been referring to the successful 2009 film *Avatar*. Although it was clearly science fiction, it made not-so-subtle references to the destruction of rain forests, the treatment of Native Americans, respect for nature, use of military force, technology, and the environmental movement.

Show Figure 6.1 to anyone and ask, "What is this?" They'll probably say, "A horse," but they'll be wrong. Why? Because this is not a horse. Rather, it is a photograph of a horse. It represents the horse. You see, I can't ride this horse, or groom it, or feed it—because it's not real. In reality, a photographer took a picture of a horse and framed it in such a way as to include some elements (like the fence, the tree, etc.) but omitted other elements (who is holding the rope outside the frame?). Technically, this is actually a grayscale copy of a photo reproduced by a graphic artist who may have altered the framing as well.

FIGURE 6.1 What is this?

Representation also deals with who is and who is not included in media. Actress Geena Davis often speaks out on the misrepresentation of women in media. A study done by the Geena Davis Institute on Gender in Media (www.thegeenadavisinstitute.org) in conjunction with the University of Southern California recently found that male characters outnumber female characters 3 to 1 in programming aimed at children. Davis says, "We judge our value by seeing ourselves reflected in culture" ("Geena Davis," 2010).

When was the last time you saw a physically disabled person as the *lead* character in a prime time television series? If you're struggling to remember one, you're not alone. (Some of us remember when actor Raymond Burr portrayed the wheelchair-bound detective in *Ironside*, 1967–1975). Recently though, characters with various disabilities have started to show up in *Glee*, *House*, *Covert Affairs*, *Private Practice*, and others. Young people, in particular, get their self-worth when they see themselves reflected positively in the media. What happens if they don't see themselves?

So perhaps good questions for students to consider might be Who is producing the media? Who is seen, who is not seen, and why? Ask students to think about what they see in the media: all they believe to be "accurate" and "real," "true-to-life" representations in the media. Now ask them how many of those representations are real, and how many are "mediated" experiences, altered forms of reality.

Representation Resources

How to Teach Representation, by David Buckingham
www.medienabc.org/page5/page19/page0/page0.html

Links to other resources, including recommended texts
www.frankwbaker.com/genrep.htm

Stereotypes

Africa—quick, when you read this word, what images came to mind? Did you immediately think of lions, tigers, giraffes, or tribesmen in the jungle? If you did, then you have a stereotypical view of Africa. Now, what if I showed you downtown Nairobi (Kenya) or Lagos (Nigeria) or Johannesburg (South Africa), with their towering skyscrapers and bustling city scenes? This, too, is Africa—perhaps not the Africa you have been exposed to. The media that we've experienced and consumed over our lifetimes has included many of the former images and excluded the latter— so we remember those images and have a stereotyped understanding of what Africa is. Think about the following people and some of their attributes: the nerdy teen, the mad scientist, the brilliant economist, the happy housewife, the rich banker, the ditsy blonde, the sleazy car salesman, the jock athlete, the lazy coworker, the terrorist Middle Eastener, the criminal Italian. Each of these are also stereotypes perpetrated by the media. And when used over time (over and over again), they become commonplace and accepted by the audience. But they should not be.

Activity

Have students comb through newspapers, magazines, and websites, identifying examples of stereotypical images. Ask them, How can teaching media literacy and debunking media stereotypes improve their view of the world and the people that live in it? Find links to more lesson plans, reading, recommended books, and more at www.frankwbaker.com/stereotypes.

Standards That Address Stereotypes

Language Arts Reading and Viewing Standards

McREL Reading Standard 6. Uses skills and strategies to read a variety of literary texts

Level III (Grades 6–8)

4. Understands elements of character development (e.g., character traits and motivations; stereotypes; relationships between character and plot development; development of characters through their words, speech patterns, thoughts, actions, narrator's description, and interaction with other characters; how motivations are revealed)

McREL Viewing Standard 9. Uses viewing skills and strategies to understand and interpret visual media

Level III (Grades 6-8)

4. Understands the use of stereotypes and biases in visual media (e.g., distorted representations of society; imagery and stereotyping in advertising; elements of stereotypes such as physical characteristics, manner of speech, beliefs and attitudes)

Level IV (Grades 9-12)

5. Uses strategies to analyze stereotypes in visual media (e.g., recognizes stereotypes that serve the interests of some groups in society at the expense of others; identifies techniques used in visual media that perpetuate stereotypes)

Source: Selected standards reprinted by permission of McREL from *Content Knowledge: A Compendium of Standards and Benchmarks for K–12 Education.*

Bias

Bias can be one of the most difficult concepts for students to define, identify and understand. Most of the bias we hear about revolves around "news media bias," which can be good for exploration and analysis. Consider the following definition of bias from media professor Ladislaus Semali (2002):

> Bias is manifest in texts when authors present particular values as if they were universal. For example, bias can be conveyed in the media through the selection of stories, sequence, and slant in newscasts; the placement or omission of stories in newspapers; who is interviewed and left out in radio or television talk shows and news programs; the advertisements on web pages, television, magazines, radio shows targeted at specific audiences; the lyrics of commercial jingles and popular music, and the images displayed with them in broadcast commercials and music videos; the goals, procedures, and the rules of video games. (para. 13)

One thing that many students may not recognize is that bias can be both in the text and in themselves. We approach media texts with our own internal biases. It will be important for students to examine their own biases at the same time that they look for bias in a written or nonprint text. Fairness & Accuracy in Reporting (FAIR) offers the backgrounder, "How to Detect Bias in News Media." I recommend you download this article, which can be found at www.fair.org/index.php?page=121, as a handout for your students.

Standards That Address Bias

Language Arts Writing, Listening and Speaking, and Viewing Standards

McREL Writing Standard 4. Gathers and uses information for research purposes

Level IV (Grades 9-12)

4. Uses a variety of criteria to evaluate the validity and reliability of primary and secondary source information (e.g., the motives and perspectives of the author; credibility of author and sources; date of publication; use of logic, propaganda, bias, and language; comprehensiveness of evidence; strengths and limitations of the source relative to audience and purpose)

Standards That Address Bias *(Continued)*

McREL Reading Standard 7. Uses skills and strategies to understand and interpret a variety of informational texts

Level IV (Grades 9-12)

4. Uses a variety of criteria to evaluate the clarity and accuracy of information (e.g., author's bias, author's expertise, authenticity, clarity of purpose, consistency, effectiveness of organizational pattern, logic of arguments, validity of reasoning, propaganda techniques, authenticity, appeal to friendly or hostile audience, effective modes of persuasion)

McREL Listening and Speaking Standard 8. Uses listening and speaking strategies for different purposes

Level III (Grades 6-8)

8. Evaluates strategies used by speakers in oral presentations (e.g., persuasive techniques, verbal messages supported by nonverbal techniques, effect of word choice, use of slanted or biased material)

McREL Viewing Standard 9. Uses viewing skills and strategies to understand and interpret visual media

Level III (Grades 6-8)

4. Understands the use of stereotypes and biases in visual media (e.g., distorted representations of society; imagery and stereotyping in advertising; elements of stereotypes such as physical characteristics, manner of speech, beliefs and attitudes)

Level IV (Grades 9-12)

2. Uses a variety of criteria (e.g., clarity, accuracy, effectiveness, bias, relevance of facts) to evaluate informational media (e.g., websites, documentaries, news programs)

Source: Selected standards reprinted by permission of McREL from *Content Knowledge: A Compendium of Standards and Benchmarks for K–12 Education.*

Test Yourself for Hidden Bias

Read about Project Implicit here:

www.tolerance.org/activity/test-yourself-hidden-bias

Take a test at Project Implicit's website and see "what may be lingering in your psyche."

https://implicit.harvard.edu/implicit

Bias Resources

Lesson Plan: Detecting Bias in a Television Newscast

www.media-literacy.ca/welcome/Ideas/Entries/2008/5/14_Media_Lit._Document_from_the__Ministry_of_Ed.__files/lesson2%20bias%20in%20TV%20newscast.pdf

"Word Choice Buffet" Activity

www.umich.edu/~newsbias/wcact.html

"Image Bias" Activities

www.umich.edu/~newsbias/img_sec.html

Additional readings, lesson plans, activities, and resources on teaching about bias

www.frankwbaker.com/bias.htm

NATIONAL EDUCATIONAL TECHNOLOGY STANDARDS

National Educational Technology Standards for Students (NETS•S)

All K–12 students should be prepared to meet the following standards and performance indicators.

1. **Creativity and Innovation**
    Students demonstrate creative thinking, construct knowledge, and develop innovative products and processes using technology. Students:

    a. apply existing knowledge to generate new ideas, products, or processes

    b. create original works as a means of personal or group expression

    c. use models and simulations to explore complex systems and issues

    d. identify trends and forecast possibilities

2. **Communication and Collaboration**
    Students use digital media and environments to communicate and work collaboratively, including at a distance, to support individual learning and contribute to the learning of others. Students:

    a. interact, collaborate, and publish with peers, experts, or others employing a variety of digital environments and media

    b. communicate information and ideas effectively to multiple audiences using a variety of media and formats

    c. develop cultural understanding and global awareness by engaging with learners of other cultures

    d. contribute to project teams to produce original works or solve problems

3. **Research and Information Fluency**
Students apply digital tools to gather, evaluate, and use information.
Students:

   a. plan strategies to guide inquiry

   b. locate, organize, analyze, evaluate, synthesize, and ethically use information from a variety of sources and media

   c. evaluate and select information sources and digital tools based on the appropriateness to specific tasks

   d. process data and report results

4. **Critical Thinking, Problem Solving, and Decision Making**
Students use critical-thinking skills to plan and conduct research, manage projects, solve problems, and make informed decisions using appropriate digital tools and resources. Students:

   a. identify and define authentic problems and significant questions for investigation

   b. plan and manage activities to develop a solution or complete a project

   c. collect and analyze data to identify solutions and make informed decisions

   d. use multiple processes and diverse perspectives to explore alternative solutions

5. **Digital Citizenship**
Students understand human, cultural, and societal issues related to technology and practice legal and ethical behavior. Students:

   a. advocate and practice the safe, legal, and responsible use of information and technology

   b. exhibit a positive attitude toward using technology that supports collaboration, learning, and productivity

   c. demonstrate personal responsibility for lifelong learning

   d. exhibit leadership for digital citizenship

6. **Technology Operations and Concepts**
Students demonstrate a sound understanding of technology concepts, systems, and operations. Students:

   a. understand and use technology systems

   b. select and use applications effectively and productively

   c. troubleshoot systems and applications

   d. transfer current knowledge to the learning of new technologies

National Educational Technology Standards for Teachers (NETS•T)

All classroom teachers should be prepared to meet the following standards and performance indicators.

1. **Facilitate and Inspire Student Learning and Creativity**
    Teachers use their knowledge of subject matter, teaching and learning, and technology to facilitate experiences that advance student learning, creativity, and innovation in both face-to-face and virtual environments. Teachers:

    a. promote, support, and model creative and innovative thinking and inventiveness

    b. engage students in exploring real-world issues and solving authentic problems using digital tools and resources

    c. promote student reflection using collaborative tools to reveal and clarify students' conceptual understanding and thinking, planning, and creative processes

    d. model collaborative knowledge construction by engaging in learning with students, colleagues, and others in face-to-face and virtual environments

2. **Design and Develop Digital-Age Learning Experiences and Assessments**
    Teachers design, develop, and evaluate authentic learning experiences and assessments incorporating contemporary tools and resources to maximize content learning in context and to develop the knowledge, skills, and attitudes identified in the NETS•S. Teachers:

    a. design or adapt relevant learning experiences that incorporate digital tools and resources to promote student learning and creativity

    b. develop technology-enriched learning environments that enable all students to pursue their individual curiosities and become active participants in setting their own educational goals, managing their own learning, and assessing their own progress

c. customize and personalize learning activities to address students' diverse learning styles, working strategies, and abilities using digital tools and resources

d. provide students with multiple and varied formative and summative assessments aligned with content and technology standards and use resulting data to inform learning and teaching

3. **Model Digital-Age Work and Learning**
    Teachers exhibit knowledge, skills, and work processes representative of an innovative professional in a global and digital society. Teachers:

a. demonstrate fluency in technology systems and the transfer of current knowledge to new technologies and situations

b. collaborate with students, peers, parents, and community members using digital tools and resources to support student success and innovation

c. communicate relevant information and ideas effectively to students, parents, and peers using a variety of digital-age media and formats

d. model and facilitate effective use of current and emerging digital tools to locate, analyze, evaluate, and use information resources to support research and learning

4. **Promote and Model Digital Citizenship and Responsibility**
    Teachers understand local and global societal issues and responsibilities in an evolving digital culture and exhibit legal and ethical behavior in their professional practices. Teachers:

a. advocate, model, and teach safe, legal, and ethical use of digital information and technology, including respect for copyright, intellectual property, and the appropriate documentation of sources

b. address the diverse needs of all learners by using learner-centered strategies and providing equitable access to appropriate digital tools and resources

    c.   promote and model digital etiquette and responsible social interactions related to the use of technology and information

    d.   develop and model cultural understanding and global awareness by engaging with colleagues and students of other cultures using digital-age communication and collaboration tools

5. **Engage in Professional Growth and Leadership**
Teachers continuously improve their professional practice, model lifelong learning, and exhibit leadership in their school and professional community by promoting and demonstrating the effective use of digital tools and resources. Teachers:

    a.   participate in local and global learning communities to explore creative applications of technology to improve student learning

    b.   exhibit leadership by demonstrating a vision of technology infusion, participating in shared decision making and community building, and developing the leadership and technology skills of others

    c.   evaluate and reflect on current research and professional practice on a regular basis to make effective use of existing and emerging digital tools and resources in support of student learning

    d.   contribute to the effectiveness, vitality, and self-renewal of the teaching profession and of their school and community

GLOSSARY

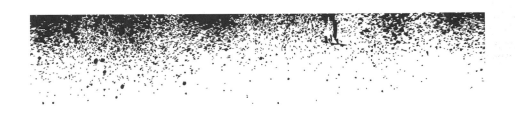

advertising (also known as **ads**, **spots**). A selling technique in which products or ideas are put forth in the media (radio, TV, film, Internet, etc.) and are aimed at a particular audience for a particular purpose.

ad watch. A column or segment (print, broadcast, or online) in which a reporter analyzes/deconstructs the words, images, and claims in a commercial (e.g., for a politician or cause).

analyze. To break something down, apply critical thinking to and study its parts.

angle. The vantage point or direction from which someone positions the camera and photographs a subject.

audience. The people who are exposed to a media message; the specific people (targeted people) most likely to see, hear, read, or be exposed to a message.

audio (**sound**). Everything one hears in a media message. It can include narration, music, sound effects.

bias. A prejudice. A personal inclination or tendency, especially one preventing unprejudiced consideration.

Bloom's Taxonomy. A hierarchy of question stems, designed in the 1950s by a committee chaired by Benjamin Bloom, to help teachers guide their students through the learning process (from lower order thinking skills, LOTS, through higher order thinking skills, HOTS).

body image. A subjective picture of one's own physical appearance established both by self-observation and by noting the reactions of others. By permission. From *Merriam-Webster's Collegiate Dictionary, 11th Edition* ©*2011* by Merriam-Webster, Incorporated (www.merriam-webster.com).

buzz. A term used by some to mean getting consumers to talk about or spread information about an item, ad, celebrity, or other news.

codes. Forms and techniques used by the media, such as camera angles, sound, and lighting (technical codes) and language, dress, and actions of characters (symbolic codes).

composition. The arrangement of items within a photographic frame, viewfinder, or image.

conventions. Long-accepted ways of doing things. Through experiencing a technique over and over, an audience becomes used to the convention. There are hundreds of conventions developed over the years that audiences accept as natural. Conventions may have to do with the structure of a narrative—such as how the passing of time is shown on film and television or fading to black.

counteradvertising. A parody ad ("counter ad") in which words, images, and sound have been changed; usually pokes fun at a message or another ad for humorous purposes.

copywriter. The person who writes copy (the script) that eventually becomes a print ad or commercial.

coverline. The captions on a magazine cover

creator. The author of a media work. (See **producer**.)

critical thinking. The intellectually disciplined process of actively and skillfully conceptualizing, applying, analyzing, synthesizing, and/or evaluating information gathered from, or generated by, observation, experience, reflection, reasoning, or communication, as a guide to belief and action (National Council for Excellence in Critical Thinking, 1987; www.criticalthinking.org/aboutCT/define_critical_thinking.cfm).

critical viewing. Applying critical thinking skills to visual messages, typically moving images—television and film.

deconstruct. To take something apart.

demographic. The physical and statistical characteristics of a human population, such as age, sex, marital status, family size, education, geographic location, and occupation, used especially to identify markets.

digital manipulation. The use of computer software (such as Photoshop) to alter an image.

dissolve. A gradual superimposing of one motion-picture or television shot upon another on a screen. By permission. From *Merriam-Webster's Collegiate Dictionary, 11th Edition* ©2011 by Merriam-Webster, Incorporated (www.merriam-webster.com).

docudrama. A blending of documentary and drama as film.

documentary (doc). A factually accurate movie, television, or radio piece based on or re-creating an actual event, life story, or era containing no fictional elements.

editing (also **video editing**, **film editing**). The cutting and joining together of video (or film) clips into a single strip. There are many ways to edit transitions from one shot to another; the cut is the simplest edit. (See also **dissolve**.)

establishing shot. A wide-angle view at the beginning of a film or video that shows the location and time of the action.

eyeballs. The specific audience an advertiser wants to reach.

focus. A photographic term to define the clarity or blurriness of an image.

framing. 1. How one constructs a photo, for example, in a camera viewfinder (deciding what to include and what to omit); 2. How media choose to explain/describe/present an issue, sometimes omitting certain important information.

gatekeeper. The function of most news organizations and how they select and control what is (and what is not) printed and/or broadcast to news audiences.

genre. A kind or type of media with its own kinds of conventions—language, characteristic signs, and sign systems.

Glogster. An online tool that allows users to create interactive posters called glogs.

kicker (or **kicker line**). In journalism, the first few words or sentence leading into a story, set in larger or bolder type than the body text of the story.

language of moving images. The tools and techniques of filmmakers, including cameras, lighting, audio, editing, setting, and actors.

light/lighting. Either natural (e.g., sun) or artificial (studio lights) used to photograph a subject or set for film or video.

masthead. The main title section and name at the front of a publication.

media (also **mass media**). The plural of (mass) medium.

media literacy. The ability to understand how the media work, how they convey meaning. Media literacy also involves critical thinking about media messages—the ability to access, analyze, and create media messages. "Media literacy empowers people to be both critical thinkers and creative producers of an increasingly wide range of messages using image, language, and sound. It is the skillful application of literacy skills to media and technology messages" (NAMLE, 2000).

medium. A medium is something we use when we want to communicate indirectly with other people, rather than in person or by face-to-face contact … television, the cinema, video, radio, photography, advertising, newspapers and magazines, recorded music, computer games and the Internet (Buckingham, 2003, p. 1).

metaphor. A figure of speech in which a word or phrase is applied in order to suggest a likeness or analogy between two different kinds of objects or ideas.

moving images. A phrase that applies to television and motion pictures (film/video).

narrative. The plot, the story, how it is told, and how it unfolds.

news literacy. The ability to use critical thinking skills to judge the reliability and credibility of news reports, whether they come via print, television, or the Internet (Schneider, 2009, para. 20).

nonprint texts. All texts that are not written (e.g., photographs, radio, television, film).

parody. To poke fun at something by creating a humorous version of it, which may include exaggerations.

perspective. A viewpoint from which one sees or interprets something.

photo op (short for **photo opportunity**). A prearranged, choreographed event designed to get the press/media to document/capture someone in a positive light. The term is often used to refer to political candidates.

point of view (or **POV**). (See **perspective**.)

producer. Someone who creates media.

production. The resulting product of a media work.

propaganda. Ideas, facts, or allegations spread deliberately and systematically to manipulate an audience's thoughts and behavior to further the propagandist's cause or to damage an opposing cause.

propaganda techniques. (See **techniques of persuasion**.)

rating. The estimated size of a TV audience watching a particular program at a particular time, expressed as a percentage.

representation. The process by which a constructed media text stands for, symbolizes, describes, or represents people, places, events, or ideas that are real and have an existence outside the text (Boles, 1994).

script. The formal, written plan for a media production.

selling line. The line near the masthead that usually contains what the magazine is about.

screenplay. A script written for film or television.

share of audience. The percentage of TV sets tuned to a certain program at a given time.

slogan. A word or phrase created by advertising and marketing people that they hope consumers will connect with their product or idea.

stereotype. An exaggerated belief, image, or distorted truth about a person or group—a generalization that allows for little or no individual differences or social variation. Stereotypes are based on images in mass media, or reputations passed on by parents, peers and other members of society. Stereotypes can be positive or negative (Teaching Tolerance, n.d., para. 4).

subtext. The underlying meaning of a message, which is not always apparent.

symbol. Something used to represent something else.

symbolism. The practice (or art) of representing things by symbols, especially by investing things with a symbolic meaning or character.

target audience. (See **audience**; see also **eyeballs**.)

target marketing. Concentrating marketing efforts on a small number of specific, key market segments (audiences).

technique. A method or tool used to create parts of a media message.

techniques of persuasion. Any number of methods used to sway opinion or persuade an audience into thinking or believing something or someone.

urban legend. Modern folklore with an unsubstantiated, usually frightening, outcome.

video. Everything seen in a moving image media message.

video clips. Selected snippets of TV programs, commercials, documentaries, or films.

visual literacy. The ability to both read and write visual information; the ability to learn visually; to think and solve problems in the visual domain (Gray, 2008).

visual representation. An image that stands for an idea, an event, or a person.

weasel words (weasely words). Misleading words or phrases, such as *acts, as much as, better, best, can be, enriched, extra special, fortified, good, great, helps, looks like, perfect, real bargain, superior, tackles, top quality, variety of uses, up to,* and *virtually.*

REFERENCES

Association for Media Literacy. (1989). *Media literacy resource guide.* Toronto, ON, Canada: Ontario Ministry of Education.

Barlow, M. (2011, March/April). Cinematic magic: Using film in class. *NEA Today*, p. 42.

Beiler, D. (Writer). (c1986). *The classics of political television advertising.* [Video recording]. In Campaign Elections, Inc., teacher's guide. Garden City, NY: Focus Media, Inc.

Bloom, B. S. (1956). *Taxonomy of educational objectives, handbook I: The cognitive domain.* New York, NY: David McKay Co.

Boles, D. (1994, Summer). The language of media literacy: A glossary of terms. *Mediacy* (newsletter of Ontario's Association for Media Literacy), *16*(3). Retrieved from www.media-awareness.ca/english/resources/educational/ teaching_backgrounders/media_literacy/glossary_media_literacy.cfm

Bowker, J. (Ed.). (1991). *Secondary media education: A curriculum statement.* London, UK: British Film Institute.

Breuer, I., & Napthine, M. (2008). *Persuasive language in media texts.* Elsternwick, Victoria, Australia: Insight Publications.

Brigham, K. (2002). Decoding visual news content. Retrieved from http:// katebrigham.com/thesis/forMIT/Interface.htm

Bristor, V. J., & Drake, S. V. (1994). Linking the language arts and content areas through visual technology. *T.H.E. Journal, 22*(2), 74–78.

Buckingham, D. (2001). *Media education: A global strategy for development.* A policy paper prepared for UNESCO. London, UK: Institute of Education, University of London.

Buckingham, D. (2003). *Questioning the media: A guide for students.* Paris, France: UNESCO. Retrieved from www.amarc.org/documents/articles/ buckingham_guide.pdf; also available from How to teach representation, www.medienabc.org/page5/page19/page0/page0.html

Burke, J. (2007). *The English teacher's companion: A complete guide to classroom, curriculum, and the profession* (3rd ed.). Portsmouth, NH: Heinemann.

Burns, M., & Martinez, D. (2002). The people's choice: Digital imagery and the art of persuasion. Austin, TX: Southwest Educational Development Laboratory. Retrieved from http://web.archive.org/web/20040105032819/www.southcentralrtec.org/alt/files/people%27schoice/17+Art+of+Persuasion.pdf

Carpenter, E., & McLuhan, M. (Eds.). (1960). *Explorations in communication: An anthology.* Boston, MA: Beacon Press.

Center for Media Literacy. (2003). *Teacher's/leader's orientation guide.* Malibu, CA: Author. Retrieved from www.medialit.org/sites/default/files/mlk_orientationguide.pdf

Center for Media Literacy. (2009). *Media Lit Kit.* Malibu, CA: Author. Retrieved from www.medialit.org/sites/default/files/mlk_orientationguide.pdf

Churches, A. (2008, April 1). Bloom's taxonomy blooms digitally. *Technology & Learning.* Retrieved from www.techlearning.com/article/8670

College Board. (2006). College Board standards for college success. New York, NY: Author. Retrieved from www.collegeboard.com/prod_downloads/about/association/academic/english-language-arts_cbscs.pdf

Considine, D. M. (2010, April). This they believe? Adolescents, advertising, and critical thinking skills. *Middle Ground*, 13(4), 14–15. Available at www.nmsa.org/Publications/MiddleGround/Articles/April2010/tabid/2164/Default.aspx

Considine, D. M., & Haley, G. E. (1999). *Visual messages: Integrating imagery into instruction.* Santa Barbara, CA: Libraries Unlimited.

Costanzo, W. (1997). *To kill a mockingbird: Then and now: A 35th anniversary celebration: Looking closely at the film.* [Teacher study guide]. Manassas, VA: Prince William Network. Retrieved April 23, 2011, from http://library.thinkquest.org/12111/SG/SG8.html

Crowley, M., & Goldman, D. (2009). *08: A graphic diary of the campaign trail.* New York, NY: Three Rivers Press.

Daly, J. (2004, September 14). Life on the screen: Visual literacy in education. *Edutopia.* Retrieved from www.edutopia.org/life-screen

Danielson, D., & Braun, D. (2005, March 8). Shark "photo of the year" is e-mail hoax. *National Geographic News.* Retrieved from http://news. nationalgeographic.com/news/2002/08/0815_020815_photooftheyear.html

Daunic, R. (2010, May 23). May 2010 M-passioned member: Jacob Burns Film Center. National Association for Media Literacy Education (NAMLE). Retrieved from http://namle.net/2010/05/23/may-2010-m-passioned-member-jacob-burns-film-center

DiCamillo, K. (2001). *Because of Winn-Dixie.* Somerville, MA: Candlewick Press.

D'sa, B. (2005). Social studies in the dark: Using docudramas to teach history. *Social Studies. 96*(1), 9–13.

Eisner, W. (2008.) *Comics and sequential art: Principles and practices from the legendary cartoonist.* New York, NY: WW Norton & Company.

Flanagin, J., & Metzger, M. (2010). *Kids and credibility: An empirical examination of youth, digital media use, and information credibility.* Cambridge, MA: MIT Press. Retrieved from http://mitpress.mit.edu/books/full_pdfs/ Kids_and_Credibility.pdf

Frank, S. (2007, February/March). Fade in: How and why to write a screenplay. *Writing! Weekly Reader 14+.*

Friedman, W. (2002, June 17). New futuristic movie contains real futuristic ads. *Advertising Age.* Retrieved April 15, 2011, from http://adage.com/article/ news/futuristic-movie-real-futuristic-ads/34817/

Geena Davis, Jackie Speier speak out on bias against women. (2010, May 11). *SF Appeal online newspaper.* Retrieved May 4, 2011, from http://sfappeal. com/alley/2010/05/geena-davis-jackie-speer-speak-out-on-bias-against-women.php

Golden, J. (2006). *Reading in the reel world: Teaching documentaries and other nonfiction texts.* Urbana, IL: National Council of Teachers of English.

Gray, D. (2008, May 22). Why PowerPoint rules the business world. [Blog post]. Retrieved from www.davegrayinfo.com/2008/05/22/ why-powerpoint-rules-the-business-world

Hobbs, R. (2007). Reading the media in high school: Media literacy in high school English. New York, NY: Teachers College Press.

International Society for Technology in Education (ISTE). (2000). *National Educational Technology Standards for Students: Connecting curriculum and technology.* Eugene, OR: Author.

International Society for Technology in Education (ISTE). (2008). *National Educational Technology Standards for Teachers* (2nd ed.). Eugene, OR: Author.

International Society for Technology in Education (ISTE). (2007). *National Educational Technology Standards for Students* (2nd ed.). Eugene, OR: Author.

Jacobson, S., & Colon, E. (2006). *The 9-11 Report: A graphic adaptation.* New York, NY: Hill and Wang.

Johnson, L. F., Levine, A., & Smith, R. S. (2009). *2009 Horizon report: The K12 edition.* Austin, TX: The New Media Consortium. Retrieved from http://wp.nmc.org/horizon-k12-2009/chapters/critical-challenges

Johnson, L. F., Levine, A., Smith, R. S., & Stone, S. (2010). *2010 Horizon report: K12 edition.* Austin, TX: The New Media Consortium. Retrieved from http://wp.nmc.org/horizon-k12-2010/chapters/challenges

Jolls, T., & Grande, D. (2005). Project Smartart: A case study in elementary school medium literacy and arts education. *Arts Education Policy Review, 107*(1), 25–30. First draft retrieved from www.medialit.org/reading-room/project-smartart-case-study-elementary-school-media-literacy-and-arts-education

Kaplan, D. (1986). *Television and the classroom.* New York, NY: Knowledge Industry Publications.

Kendall, J. (2011). *Content knowledge: A compendium of standards and benchmarks for K–12 education.* [Online edition]. Retrieved from www.mcrel.org/standards-benchmarks

Kubey, R., & Baker, F. (1999, October 27). Has media literacy found a curricular foothold? *Education Week, 19,* 56.

Kilbourne, J. (2000). *Can't buy my love: How advertising changes the way we think and feel.* New York, NY: Touchstone.

Lenhart, A., Ling, R., Campbell, S., & Purcell, K. (2010, April 20). Teens and mobile phones. Pew Internet and American Life Project, Pew Research Center. Retrieved April 8, 2011, from www.pewinternet.org/Press-Releases/2010/Teens-and-Mobile-Phones.aspx

Lyga, A. (2006, March 1). Graphic novels for (really) young readers. *School Library Journal.* Retrieved April 14, 2011, from www.schoollibraryjournal.com/article/CA6312463.html?q=Graphic+novels+for+%28really%29+young+readers

Marks, D. (2009). Media literacy project. Literacy, Technology, and Instruction, a course taught in summer 2009 at Appalachian State University. Retrieved from http://sites.google.com/site/ci3850summer09/Home/media-literacy-project/tap-questions

Masterman, L. (1985). *Teaching the media.* London, UK: Comedia.

media literacy. (2000). National Association for Media Literacy Education (NAMLE). Retrieved July 22, 2011, from http://namle.net/publications/media-literacy-definitions

Mihailidis, P. (2009). Beyond cynicism: Media education and civic learning outcomes in the university. *International Journal of Media and Learning, 1*(3), 19–31.

National Association for Media Literacy Education (NAMLE). (2000). Media literacy defined. Retrieved July 22, 2011, from http://namle.net/publications/media-literacy-definitions

National Board for Professional Teaching Standards. (2003). *Adolescence and young adulthood/English language arts standards.* Retrieved from www.nbpts.org/userfiles/File/aya_ela_standards.pdf

National Council of Teachers of English. (1996). Position statement. Resolution on viewing and visually representing as forms of literacy. Approved at the 1996 NCTE annual business meeting in Chicago, IL. Retrieved from www.ncte.org/positions/statements/visualformofliteracy

National Council of Teachers of English/International Reading Association. (1996). *Standards for the English language arts.* Retrieved from www.ncte. org/library/NCTEFiles/Resources/Books/Sample/StandardsDoc.pdf

National Health Education Standards, Joint Committee on. (2007). *National health education standards: Achieving excellence* (2nd ed.). Atlanta, GA: American Cancer Society. Retrieved from www.cdc.gov/HealthyYouth/ SHER/standards/index.htm

New Media Consortium. (2005). A *global imperative: The report of the 21st century literacy summit.* Austin, TX: Author. Retrieved from http://archive. nmc.org/pdf/Global_Imperative.pdf

O'Donnell, L., & Deas, M. (2009). *Media meltdown: A graphic guide adventure.* Custer, WA: Orca.

Ogle, D. (1986). K-W-L: A teaching model that develops active reading of expository text. *The Reading Teacher, 39*(6), 564–570.

Ontario Ministry of Education. (1989). *Media literacy resource guide.* Toronto, ON, Canada: Author.

Paley Center for Media. (n.d.). *The fine art of persuasion: Television & advertising.* New York, NY: author. Retrieved from assets.paleycenter.org/assets/ education/classPDFs/artpersuasion.pdf

Pungente SJ, J. J., & O'Malley, M. (1999). *More than meets the eye: Watching television watching us.* The Association for Media Literacy, Toronto, ON, Canada: McClelland & Stewart. Retrieved from www.medialit.org/ reading-room/canadas-key-concepts-media-literacy

Rideout, V., Foehr, U., & Roberts, D. (2010). *Generation M2: Media in the lives of 8- to 18-year-olds.* The Kaiser Family Foundation. Retrieved from www.kff. org/entmedia/upload/8010.pdf

Riesland, E. (2005). Visual literacy and the classroom. *New Horizons for Learning.* Retrieved from http://education.jhu.edu/newhorizons/strategies/ topics/literacy/articles/visual-literacy-and-the-classroom/index.html

Schewe, J. (2005, April 3). Kate doesn't like Photoshop—Digital ethics. PhotoshopNews.com. Retrieved April 8, 2011, from http://photoshopnews. com/2005/04/03/kate-doesnt-like-photoshop

Schneider, H. (2009, March). Opening remarks, day two. The 2009 News Literacy Conference, Stony Brook University, Stony Brook, NY. Retrieved April 23, 2011, from www.newsliteracyconference.com/content/wp-content/ uploads/2009/07/NL-Conference-Report.pdf also retrieved from www. newsliteracyconference.com/content/wp-content/uploads/2009/07/ NL-Conference-Report.doc

Semali, L. (2002, December/January). Crossing the information highway: The web of meanings and bias in global media. *Reading Online*, 6(5). Retrieved from www.readingonline.org/newliteracies/lit_index.asp?HREF=semali3/ index.html

Share, J., Thoman, E., & Jolls, T. (2002–2011). *Five key questions that can change the world: Classroom activity guide with 25 plans for K–12 media literacy.* Malibu, CA: Center for Media Literacy. Retrieved from www.medialit.org/ five-key-questions-can-change-world

Shepherd, R. (1992). Elementary media education: The perfect curriculum. Adapted from *English Quarterly*, 25(2–3). Retrieved from www.media-awareness.ca/english/resources/educational/teaching_backgrounders/ media_literacy/perfect_curriculum_1.cfm

Singer, N. (2010, May 2). Shoppers who can't have secrets. *The New York Times.* Retrieved from www.nytimes.com

Strong, E. K. (1925). Theories of selling. *Journal of Applied Psychology, 9*, 75–86.

Taylor, J. (2011, May 6). Teaching with political & editorial cartoons. *The Change Agent: An Adult Education Newspaper for Social Justice*. Retrieved from www.nelrc.org/changeagent/cartoons.htm

Teaching Tolerance, A Project of the Southern Poverty Law Center. (n.d.). *Test yourself for hidden bias*. Montgomery, AL: Author. Retrieved from www. tolerance.org/activity/test-yourself-hidden-bias

Thoman, E. (1993). *Skills & strategies for media education*. Alexandria, VA: Association for Supervision and Curriculum Development. Retrieved from www.medialit.org/reading-room/skills-strategies-media-education

Thoman, E., & Jolls, T. (2003). *Literacy for the 21st century: An overview and orientation guide to media literacy education*. Malibu, CA: Center for Media Literacy. Available from www.medialit.org/literacy-21st-century

Thompson, L. (2003). *Key ingredients: America by food*. [Teacher's guide]. Washington, DC: Smithsonian Institution. Retrieved April 20, 2011, from www.agclassroom.org/teacher/pdf/key_ingredients.pdf

UK Film Council. (n.d.). *Film: 21st century literacy: A strategy for film education across the UK. London, UK: 21st Century Literacy*. Retrieved from www.ukfilmcouncil.org.uk/media/pdf/g/t/Film-21st_Century_Literacy.pdf

Winton, E. (2010, March 10). Beyond the textbook: Documentaries as a tool for teaching. *Art Threat*. Retrieved from http://artthreat.net/2010/03/documentaries-teaching-tool

Wright, J. S., Winter, W. L., Zeigler, S. K., & O'Dea, P. N. (1982). *Advertising*. New York, NY: McGraw-Hill.

Yousman, B. (2006). Asking the right questions: The power of media literacy. Quoted by A. Hornaday. (2006, August 6). Chill out, Mom. *The Washington Post*. Retrieved from www.washingtonpost.com/wp-dyn/content/article/2006/08/04/AR2006080400226.html

INDEX

Page references followed by *f* indicate figures.
Page references in *italics* indicate sidebars.

E

F

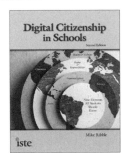